my girlosophy

anthea paul

How to write your own life

ALLEN&UNWIN

contents

Dedication

There is a long lineage of writers who have traveled to far-flung corners of the globe and kept journals, thereby enlightening the rest of us with their thoughts, experiences and understanding. But it's a risky business. Travel, of course, usually involves a level of uncertainty of some sort, and writing has always been considered a dicey occupation, due mostly to the associated lifestyle and financial risks. However, in the past decade especially, the stakes have been raised to the limit – now the risk of being a writer or journalist is frequently a physical one.

All over the world, journalists and writers are routinely threatened, arrested, interrogated, captured, held hostage, and sometimes executed. Some have simply disappeared without a trace, presumably killed. Many journalists, photojournalists, reporters, and writers have lost their lives just for doing their job: pursuing the truth. Their sacrifice is of the highest order.

In monitoring those who would suppress the rights of others - whether human, animal or environmental - and by bringing perpetrators to account in the global public arena, writers and reporters show us real courage. What they do is of crucial importance in a media-based world where spin rules.

This book is dedicated to the brave individuals who continue to speak up despite the considerable personal danger, and to those who no longer can.
Reporters without borders (Reporters Sans Frontiers)

Article 19

Everyone has the right to freedom of
des freedom to hold opinions witho
impart information and ideas throu

on and expression; this right inclu-
erference and to seek, receive and
media and regardless of frontiers.

Universal Declaration of Human Rights, Article 19

introduction

Welcome to **my girlosophy – how to write your own life.** For those girlosophers all over the world who have been following the story so far, this is the seventh title in the **girlosophy** series. Lucky number seven ... rhymes with heaven! And to me it is numerologically auspicious. Seven is the number that reflects the spiritual pursuits or of "going within", a driving principle of the girlosophy series to date. But in this outing, it is what you are going to write as a result of diving in that is of the most importance. The focus here is completely on you: your thoughts, your communication with your Self, and the spirit within you.

So, what is **my girlosophy?** Well, for one thing, it's a book about writing – duh! Less obviously perhaps, it's a book about discovery: mapping your internal journey while you tread the external one. **True to girlo form, it's about the discovery of you (FOR you) and of your Self (FOR yourself).**

It is clear we navigate our lives more skillfully and effectively by knowing the landscape of our own psychology. And although you may still be somewhat of a stranger in your inner paradise, it is my hope that within these pages you will find that "the doors of perception" will kick open for you. The good old Buddhists are fond of saying: **"The way in is the way out"** – it seems especially fitting for this book.

To really get the most out of **my girlosophy**, you don't need to become a Pulitzer Prize-winning writer – well not yet anyway! There is no pressure. In **my girlosophy**, it's all about the process of delving deep and just seeing what comes up, or out, onto the page.

The discovery of writing gives you more self-reliance – you can write what's going on for you in your journal instead of always downloading on friends and family. Writing can become your first port of call when you need to release something, or perhaps even when you need to buy some time before you react. Writing forces you to THINK rather than react. It makes you face words on a page that can be truly understood only with a **"cool head and a warm heart"**. Writing shows you where your negative patterns are and – through subsequent reflection – helps you gain the power to make real changes in your life.

> "We are people who want to take reality and make it our own inside our journals. Whether we do it in a physical, mental or spiritual realm is left up to the journal-er."
> Jolee Moffett
> The Baghdad Diaries Project

Among other things, writing is invariably a journey for the participants – writer and reader – in the process. And so it is in this spirit that the journey within begins. Initially it will be for you, the reader; later it will be for you, the writer. Here we'll be taking both the abstract and the conceptual and then applying them to your world.

From here on, it's all about your personal (R)evolution.

o dig deep

The journey
is the destination

"But right now I just feel stagnant and a bit lost in my head. We'll probably leave around June 10th with some cameras, journals, skateboards, sleeping bags, a few road maps and only two rules: no hotels and no cell phones."

Jon Rose, from Towards Miles:
Observations of an American Passage

In order to discover anything in life, whether intellectual, emotional or physical, you need a spirit of adventure, an enthusiasm for exploration, a willingness to be led, and the ability to take the initiative. You also need to be able to handle rejection, failure, disappointment, success, surprise, and confusion.

When seeking adventure (or mystery and magic!) of any description, you also need to cope with things going (a) in an unanticipated direction, or (b) horribly wrong; and being able to flow with either scenario. In many respects, writing is exactly the same. You may not end up anywhere near where you thought you were heading, but you can cover a lot of miles while you're lost!

On any quest, there is normally some sort of goal involved (a Holy Grail if you will), however, put aside all notions of achievement or of being entirely goal-oriented. Just for the time being.

To be an artist of life – and writers are always such – you need to take the highs and the lows and view them all in a macro, big-picture sense. **It's all about the search.**

It's your personal
"Discovery Channel" ...

Let's simply imagine the wonder and thrill of just taking the next corner without any preconceptions about what will happen. In our writing, let's explore. But let's do it without putting any time constraints in place, and without the fear of NOT getting anywhere. For that is what the journey of writing needs to be. Writing just for the thrill and freedom of it is one of the most intensely challenging, satisfying, and liberating things you can do. Nothing can compare to the wonder of finding that which lies within you.

As any explorer knows, the flipside to any adventure is a certain degree of preparation. And in order to prepare to write or to get something positive from the process, you need to bring some sort of effort to the task. Writing is a discipline and it requires as much from us. **It takes diligence to be consistent.** But more than anything it takes a good deal of tenacity to just keep banging away! As it is well known, even in professional sport, perseverance beats talent every day. Like most things in life, writing or keeping a journal is best done fairly regularly to gain the most from it. Keeping track of your tracks, so to speak, is just a great thing to do. You can check out what you were doing ages after and it will all come back to you. Who cares if what you wrote down has crossed out lines and the odd spelling mistake? The energy will still be there, fresh on the page, the same as the day you wrote it, although the meaning to you may well have changed.

It's a memory and it's a story and, best of all, IT'S ALL YOURS. And that is the point of **my girlosophy.** Here, you are simply going to do it regardless of being good, bad or mediocre!

"The journal is still my compass. Within the private confines of its cover, I translate places physical and emotional. Through its unique visual language I am not afraid to communicate honestly."
Jessica Cannon, www.daneldon.org

About my girlosophy

To start with you need to write on something. Any old exercise book, or scrap of paper will do, but it would be best if you could create a journal for you to use for life. Begin by engaging with **my girlosophy – how to write your own life**, consider the ideas and themes presented, and then work through them in your very own journal!

Rule #1: Judge not thyself!

In using the Journal, I would like to stress that it is important not to be judgmental. Being "non-judgmental" means you should try to bring your most neutral head-space to the task. **Try not to tell yourself things like: "I can't write anything, I'm hopeless ... I can't even spell." It is also not helpful to say things to yourself like: "I'm not creative or talented, why would I be able to write?" Nor: "I can't remember what happened yesterday, I can't keep a journal!"**
For the purposes of creativity, saying "NO" to yourself is a "NO-NO", and it only holds you back.

Rather, hold the attitude that it is all about trying something fun and new and sticking with it for a bit. This is what I'm really getting at when I talk about "the process".

I hope to inspire each reader with the idea that whatever is recorded within the journal's pages has the potential to become the passport to a greater understanding of who you are.

how to write your own life

Self-knowledge leads to a greater understanding of others. It's my firm belief that this is the true purpose of why we are here.

Not many people are simply gifted at writing – although they certainly exist – and even fewer of these are brilliant without any application whatsoever. I absolutely do not consider myself gifted, however, this has never prevented me from enjoying the process of writing.

The less I judge myself while I write (and about what I write) in my journal, the more I tend to flow with things and just relax. When I write in this state, I can often manifest tons of stuff without even trying, which – regardless of quality, grammar, etc. – is astonishing to re-read later.

The hidden bonus of keeping the Journal is the learning curve. The rewards are invaluable and transformational, a reminder that the greatest creativity happens when we don't judge or hold back its natural progression.

Globalgirlospeak

Researchers in the United States recently found that girls, not boys – sorry! – are "the single most important influence on the evolution of the English language" (as reported in *The Australian* news paper, 9 January 2006). Teenage girls are the most prolific journal-writers and, aided and abetted by the development of new technologies, this has the potential to shape girls as a dominant and powerful force in our global future.

It is up to us how we use this new power. Just as the confidence of becoming and being ourselves brings rewards, we should also be mindful that we should share those rewards with others. You are able to directly impact on the way you communicate with and relate to others now and in the future. It is an exciting position to be in.

Use our rich language and the largely untapped imagination at your disposal for positive personal and universal change. Practice your writing in your journals and hone your skills so that when you write to your friends and those in charge of the

Small steps cover lots of ground

planet you can communicate your thoughts well.
my girlosophy is divided into sections to enable you to begin your writing journey in comfort (and style!). The first section deals with your set-up: the things you will need to write, from your basic equipment to finding a space in which you will feel inspired. Warm-up exercises, affirmations and other hot tips will help to get you in the right vibe.

At this stage, it is all about you building yourself up to a level of self-discipline where the

momentum kicks in and your writing flows more naturally as a result. It may feel a bit strange and unnatural at first, but in time and with practice you will see that **small steps can lead to a giant leap.**

The sections that follow deal with your voice, themes to write about and different writing formats.

In the section devoted to helping you to find your voi
Once you find your voice in life you can use it to go out
operator. "Finding your Voice" will connect you with the
on the page. The routine of writing on a daily basis form
meditation will calm your mind and allow your creativity
preparation for writing. Like anything in life, your voic

I urge all young women to put their energies into finc
handbag or body shape. **Put the focus on having experiences and**
share them with the world and your shining personality
remind anyone what lasts longer!

The next chapter is devoted to the notion of a "theme'
interesting; some would say, easier. Diving into either a
a "stream of consciousness" or "free association" rant on
shape to a writing task.

Themes are a word or an idea that link and provide
that have a strong association and which boost imaginatio
. Words contain energy and they are powerful so
resulting work pulses with a life and spirit of its own.

Theme / n. 1. a subject of discourse;
discussion, meditation, or composition; a topi
The Macquarie Concise Dictionary, Third Edition

include a couple of methods to give you some inspiration.
to the world and be both confident and an effective
urce of your writing talent and help you to harness it
art of the process. In this section, techniques such as
surface. Meditation is a gentle and non-intrusive
will come more readily if you don't force it.

heir voice instead of worrying if they have the right
writing about them instead of accessorizing. Record your stories,
ill be your passport – not your looks. I don't need to

emes are essential and they make the writing process
ze of facts or a story using themes, or simply doing
ticular word or theme, helps to bring structure and

nsistency. Call it a vein or thread if you like. Words
d perhaps even jog memory, are at the heart of my
always wise to use them well. By using a theme, the

23

See me write ...

As readers have come to expect from **girlosophy**, there's a classic girlo element at work in this book: the all-pervasive visual referencing. In the formats section and in the "Real Girls Write!" section, we explore the visual journal format with loads of real examples.

The various formats available are canvassed as options for writing — one girlo's private diary is another's website or blog. Be wide-ranging in your productivity! Choose an outlet and explore, and then try another. Maybe you can even help to save the whales or the rainforests with your own personal blog.

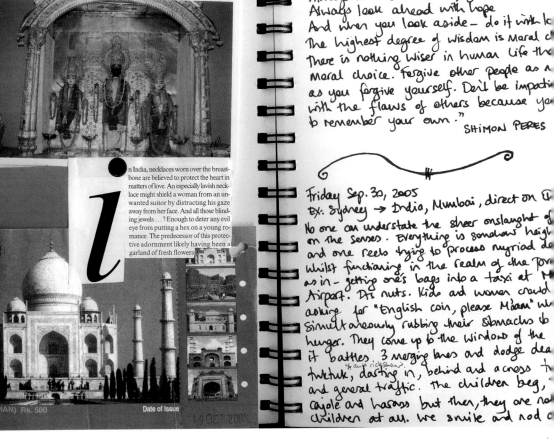

n India, necklaces worn over the breast-bone are believed to protect the heart in matters of love. An especially lavish neck-lace might shield a woman from an un-wanted suitor by distracting his gaze away from her face. And all those blind-ing jewels...? Enough to deter any evil eye from putting a hex on a young ro-mance. The predecessor of this protec-tive adornment likely having been a garland of fresh flowers

IAN) Rs. 500   Date of Issue

"Always look back with forgiveness.
Always look ahead with hope
And when you look aside — do it with lo
The highest degree of wisdom is Moral c
There is nothing wiser in human life th
Moral choice. Forgive other people as r
as you forgive yourself. Don't be impati
with the flaws of others because yo
to remember your own."
                              SHIMON PERES

Friday Sep. 30, 2005
Ex: Sydney → India, Mumbai, direct on U
No one can understate the sheer onslaught of
on the senses. Everything is somehow heigh
and one reels trying to process myriad de
whilst functioning in the realm of the for
as in — getting one's bags into a taxi at M
Airport. It's nuts. Kids and women crowd
asking for "English coin, please Maam" wr
simultaneously rubbing their stomachs to
hunger. They come up to the windows of the
it battles. 3 merging lanes and dodge dea
tuktuk, darting in, behind and across t
and general traffic. the children beg,
cajole and harass but then, they are no
children at all. We smile and nod a

But the diary has long been a favored format: think *The Basketball Diaries*, *Bridget Jones' Diary*, *The Diary of Anne Frank*, *The Andy Warhol Diaries*! A diary is illuminating in a way that an objective view of the same subject can rarely be. At its best, a diary opens a personal window to a universal viewpoint. I hope to inspire each girlo reader to create her own diary and/or scrapbook with a blank journal.

Remember, sometimes **a picture can generate ONE THOUSAND WORDS.** Be inspired by girlosopher Sam Symonds' beautiful drawings from her exquisite painted travel journal that captures her trips to Australia, Peru and Mexico. And take a look at Mel Foulkes' visual response to her world – a crayon drawing done each day to match her mood. Mel's heartfelt and simple musings on life will resonate for many.

In the "Real Girls Write!" section, you will also find excerpts of Carly Anderson's diary as she courageously charts her way through the difficult process of grief after the death of her beloved brother, Luke. We also meet Adriana Marques – a young Brazilian with a passion for living – and her massive circle of friends from many countries. Brittany Ervin, a committed Christian from the United States blogs her way to a sense of self, pondering the questions of faith as she navigates life. Brittany's voice is fresh and articulate.

Whether revealing our seemingly infinite flaws and pretensions, or blatantly reminding us how hard it is to write well, diaries are nonetheless a first and necessary step in shaping our sense of the world and our place in it.

girlosophers' Privacy Policy!

The purpose of this section is to urge all girlosophers to be careful and, at least, a little bit diplomatic when you write stuff.

This extends to what you put, well, anywhere really. Many things that should remain private, unfortunately - and embarrassingly - do not. Some people vent furiously in their journals but this can be a disaster if the journal or notebook falls into the wrong hands. It could be seriously damaging to another innocent party and land you in hot water that you may take a while to recover from.

This is especially crucial, when you are writing about other people. Try and write so that - in what has to be a worst-case scenario - if it does get read by the person you are writing about or by another (perhaps a third party with an axe to grind) you can at least still hold your head up in public.

For those of you who have seen the movie *Mean Girls*, need I say more? For those of you referencing *Bridget Jones' Diary*, we all know in real life Mark Darcy would never have come back after reading the dreadful comments about him as written by poor, dear old Bridg.

Pretty much the rule is to ask yourself, if someone else read this would it reflect badly on me? Would it be taken the wrong way or would it be hurtful to someone?

As far as possible it is best to take the high road, even in the privacy of your thoughts or journal. Try and be fair when you write about people. This is good practice for day-to-day dealings in any case.

And do take precautions: hide your journal or diary in a safe place – one that pesky younger brothers or somewhat snoopy roommates won't easily lay their mitts on, by accident or design. You certainly have a right to your privacy but don't be provocative either – people can seldom resist things they know they shouldn't be reading (especially if it is left on the kitchen table for days). Take care and for goodness sake, PUT IT AWAY. Under lock and key if needed.

The last thing you need is someone having access to your personal feelings and innermost thoughts if they do not necessarily have your best interests at heart or the maturity to be able to deal with it (in the case of younger brothers or sisters!).

And this being girlo, the reverse applies too. Respect the privacy of others. If your sister, mum or roommate has a journal or some sort of diary, don't invade their privacy by trying to find it or reading it over their shoulder. Instead, respect their journey and go write in your own. Having said that ...

Lighting the shadows

"I can't say I want to go home to anyone.
I might cry if I try. Someone asks me if I'm going home.
I say I don't know where home is. They look worried.
It worries me too. How many homes do I have
to have before I feel at home?"
Lily Brett, 'Between Mexico and Poland'

I am always interested in the idea of writing as not only being a useful creative tool but in how recording words and thoughts in a written form is a direct means to increasing self-knowledge and exposing one's dark or hidden parts. Throwing light on darkness – by which I mean the hidden or shadow Self – is the only way to confront issues and create real change.

Pain and rage can serve as pathways to a new level of involvement in your own life. Once you acknowledge their existence you can transmute these powerful energies and re-harness them to serve you via new channels. You become the master of your emotions and not the slave. Use negative energy in a positive way by allowing it to help you GENERATE new creative output. When viewed this way, recording your world becomes a spiritual activity.

It is my hope that this is both the experience and the outcome for all girlosophers.

The future is the written word ...

I have received many letters and emails from my readers, some of whom are keen to be published but many who are just keen to have feedback of what they are doing creatively or to let me know how they have been inspired. I am frequently sent links to blogs, websites, online journals, and so forth, which I am always extremely delighted to receive.

Writing — as many writers, journalists and authors will attest — is truly a form of therapy. It is also — as just as many writers, journalists and authors will attest — sheer torture on occasion, probably for the same reason! What makes writing joyful, painful, rewarding, confronting, exasperating and exhilarating is invariably what we bring to the process in the first place and how we approach and/or handle ourselves when we do sit down to write.

By writing things down, we are each more likely to understand the inherent meaning with the passage of time. Writing is a clear path to "learning your Self". For this reason, I believe there is possibly no other art form or medium that can be so directly helpful to the individual in her (or his) life.

That so many girlosophers are gaining so much by reflecting on their personal worlds and sharing it with others is testimony to the power of thought – and creative energy. With **my girlosophy - how to write your own life,** I hope more readers will be similarly inspired to write things down, to record and ruminate on life, as it happens.

It is my hope that young women around the world will be inspired to get their thoughts in order, to reflect on life and to speak up!

Many things on the planet need to change and to be changed. But we seem to lack the necessary articulate and impassioned YOUNG voices we saw in the past to maintain the sense of urgency. If it's crunch time maybe it's your voice we need to hear.

My final note here is this: the only way to liberate the world is for individuals to liberate themselves first. How can we truly be free if we are carrying the weight of the past and the burdens of old? Freedom of expression is a basic platform in a real and vibrant democracy and the crucial ingredient in activating change.

The great joy of life and the beauty about being alive is that we can rewrite our own script. We should not waste this opportunity to become the best version of ourselves that we can be. It's time to do our homework. Forget about superficial Hollywood movies: we are the writer/director in our own right, in our own lives.

Accordingly, this gives us the ability to consciously decide to change at any time. This is a supreme paradigm shift. And just as individuals need to "clean up their own backyard" in the aim of maximizing potential, so must countries at large do the same. The personal is the universal.

And if the act of writing is one of personal expression, it ultimately is one of freedom. It is the ability we have to put or throw down words in our own way. We can make our own choices. On the blank page we can get to know and recreate ourselves. We can be intimate. And if we do this fearlessly and truthfully, we are able to become who we really are. In doing so, we gain the ability to bring light to and express the hidden parts of our souls in order that both we and the world-at-large may be connected anew. We become powerful and indestructible. **Our words live forever.**

That's real freedom.

Anthea Paul
Agra, India, October 2005

33

And if the act of writing is one of personal expression, it ultimately is one of freedom.... we gain the ability to bring light to and express the hidden parts of our souls in order that both we and the world-at-large may be connected anew. We become powerful and indestructible. **Our words live forever.**

why write?

Because you can, duh!

Now there's a challenge to non-believers. But you know what, you *can* write, and I will prove it to you. I believe that anyone can be creative, it's our true nature.

Creativity is not just the sole province of "Superstar Genius Artist Types". Many of us believe – are convinced, in fact – that we do not have a creative bone in our body. We believe that other people have some artistic gene which we missed out on and which gives them an advantage. Yes there are people who seem to know very early on that they are creative, and they pursue that arena to great effect and success. But these truly are the rare cases. For most of us it is more of a gradual awakening as opposed to something always felt from childhood.

Some so-called artists seem to just get by doing the same old, same old stuff. Such artists have ceased to do original things or take risks in their work. Instead they have become limited by their beliefs. For some it's even worse: they become blocked and then stay there, not creating anything at all. I'm sure you've heard of "Writer's Block", which can be "Painter's Block", "Designer's Block" and "Photographer's Block" too. There are many ways to be blocked! And you may be blocking your creativity without knowing it.

If there is such a thing as a creative gene, it may simply be that it is dormant within you. If there is no outlet for your talent, how would you even know if you have it or not? It needs to be found and expressed. And it may even need to be to be coaxed out of hiding.

No one has a monopoly on being creative, or on being an artist. The creative arts are about problems and an ability to solve them. We – you and me – are inherently creative. You can write, paint, draw, sculpt, shoot, design, or basically do whatever you decide you want to do. You can solve problems! It's about creating the opportunity to showcase what you can do.

That is why, in order to write and be creative, we must each "prepare the vessel and the spirit will descend". Much like anything else worthwhile in life, you get back what you put in.

We are all artists of life.

Getting started

Just sitting down to write – or finding or making the time to do it – can be a challenge in itself. But once you actually get to this point, the realization hits that there is nowhere to go and nothing to do but deal with the blank screen or page in front of you.

I will sometimes go to extraordinary lengths to not sit at my desk, nor indeed any place where I might write. I am capable of making any excuse: cleaning, taking the dog for a walk, telephone calls, meals to prepare ... I can be endlessly creative at times in order to avoid being creative! As I write this, I see how silly that must seem. It's what I love to do, so why the delay? Why the denial? Why the procrastination?

It all boils down to the same thing: FEAR.

It is my – probably irrational – fear that maybe I won't be able to "do it" this time. I have this fear that maybe I'll seize up halfway through and never get to the end. But mostly I think my fear is, "What's going to come out this time?!" or "Will I be able to deal with that?" or the classic fear: "Am I good enough?" Ouch!

It is ultimately my fear of the unknown, and this has a lot to do with my perception of being judged by others. But I have to admit that on the other side of this fear, I do know what is going to happen. It's the same process every time. And the fear shows me where I need to go.

It's a bit like giving birth: you know the process will require endurance, be a bit of a mess, and probably involve a good dose of pain, but at the end there will be joy and immense satisfaction.

In this section, we will get into the heart of what you need to be a writer, and the benefits of keeping journals and training yourself to write, how to overcome the dreaded "Writer's Block", and a few handy tricks to keep you in the game.

The tools of the trade

You don't need much to be a writer. A beautiful water-marked journal with a silk cord will be a lot more inspiring to fill with your bon mots than a stained notepad, but bear in mind that a blank piece of paper and a basic ballpoint pen have served many of our greatest artists.

If you prefer to use the keyboard for your navel-gazing, then make your laptop your best friend and constant companion. Many prolific writing professionals could probably not produce their work without one. But they would almost certainly, no matter what kind of writer they are – screenwriter, novelist, journalist, etc. – keep handwritten notes and journals.

I personally recommend handwriting in journals, more for the ease of reading back over stuff later. In addition, you won't risk "losing" the document that you just spent ages typing in. Hard copies rule!

Sometimes a sheath of fresh white paper and a mug full of artline pens (my favorite kind, just so you know!) is all you need to add horsepower to your output.

I like my journals to be individual, hard-bound and "project specific". I can recognize a journal individually from a trip or from a particular time in my life just from how it looks. But everyone is different: Virgin Chief Richard Branson reportedly writes in a particular kind of slender school exercise book and literally fills the bookshelves in his office with them and has done this for his entire career. Apparently, he writes in them every day, during every meeting or phone call, so he can recall every idea that he may have had.

Clearly he has had many, so this method works for him – hmmm ... write and get mega-rich, perhaps?

JOHN GRISHAM
THE BROKER
sidney sheldon
DAN BROWN
DIGITAL FORTRESS
DAN BROWN
DECEPTION POINT
THE DA VINCI CODE
Dan Brown
ANGELS DEMONS
THE ALCHEMIST
Malcolm Gladwell
MH 06

The three R's
Read, Read, Read

When you write it is incredibly helpful to spend a lot of time reading. This probably sounds like the complete opposite to what think you need to be doing. But think about it this way, Coldplay wouldn't know how to write a pop song if they didn't spend a good amount of time listening to music!

You may need to miss *The O.C.* or your other favorite television shows occasionally in order to do so, but **by reading a lot you will be inspired to write a lot.** It's true and it's that simple. It provides you with a sense of, well if J.K. Rowling can do it, so can I!

If you don't have access to a family bookshelf full of the classics, get in touch with your local library. Ask the librarian if you are unsure about where to begin, they normally are an excellent resource: a font of knowledge, and keen to see people read.

No matter what is specifically causing it, a "block" occurs when the creative vein dries up. It feels like there is nothing left in the well, and it all comes to a grinding halt. In short, you have come to an obstacle on the creative course. It may just be a temporary obstacle, preventing you from writing clearly or even having the desire to put pen to paper, but you suffer regardless.

When this happens, you usually can't pull anything together. You feel uninspired, unable to express what you want to and what you feel is within you. Above all, you feel incapable of seeing something – a letter, an article, anything – to fruition. And so the journal, paper, book or notepad sits there, day after day (or indeed year after year) not filled in, perhaps not even opened.

This is the writer's basic nightmare!

It's heavy: no pen to paper or keystroke to screen occurs. Instead fear, bitterness, recrimination, anger, sadness, regret and anxiety rule the creative slate. Without a "circuit breaker" or some kind of methodology to get you back into the game, this can indeed spell the end of the line for many would-be creators.

So, how does this happen? Why does it get to this point? Why does inspiration seem to flee, for all intents and purposes, never to be seen again?

And what, if anything, can you do about it?

the course

The Toddler's Trick

Three-year-olds have no problem expressing themselves. They can paint and draw pictures endlessly. They do not seem to have a moment's hesitation about what to put onto a canvas or a massive piece of paper. Give the tots a piece of paper and a paintbrush and they happily go straight to it, with nary a pause. Nor do they mind when they make a mess of the paint colors or tear the paper – they never judge their output.

In this respect, they are great teachers to all of us who would be creative. To a small child, the creative product is what it is, exactly the way it has turned out, whether intended or not. It looks however it looks. They are not intimidated by and nor do they have conflict with the process of creation. They are enviably free of baggage and judgment about it. That free approach invokes the same in us — as viewers we suspend our judgment and simply enjoy the spirit of their art. We don't say "Oh, you shouldn't have used that color there", or "Why did you make it so blobby in the corner?" We do not criticize. We bring our best selves to their table and we are encouraging of their every effort.

Everyone loves a child's artwork. It is successful artwork because children create with **a clear channel, a present mind and an open heart.**

We should all think and act the same way as children when it comes to the creative task of writing, in whatever form it takes. We should allow ourselves to be small children again! We should applaud our own creative efforts without thinking about it too much or falling into the trap of being self-critical. This is the key to bringing forth more.

Being kind

Too much negativity and judgment creates blockage – the opposite effect to what we would like to achieve. If you wish to tap into the rich treasure trove of your subconscious, then you must suspend any tendency to be negative about your efforts – and about your Self. Above all else, negativity stunts the natural creative and spiritual flow.

to your Self

The gift of time

Like speech, writing is individual. And what emerges when we write anything is absolutely the mark of the person. Your writing is as unique as your fingerprint! Giving yourself the time to record what is happening in your world is truly a gift that keeps on giving. You need the time to sit, the time to reflect and the time to actually write. Then there is the time to let the writing sit too.

Time is a great re-framer of the written word. By reading something long after it has been written, it can be analyzed and understood objectively. Time is a key factor when you write. It shows you exactly what you were thinking and why. Maybe you'll be able to see where you could have acted or reacted differently – say with more compassion or perhaps just without losing your temper! Maybe a pattern of behavior that is holding you back is revealed by the words. Setting aside regular time to write, and to read back what you have written, is time well spent.

Try this exercise. # JUST FOR FUN

1. Find a piece of blank paper. Any size will do, but try to make it at least A4 (standard photocopy size).
2. Grab a few different colored pens and pencils, the more the merrier.
3. Rest the paper on top of something so you can write on it easily (a magazine or back of a large notepad works here; telephone books are good too).
4. Take this stuff with you and find a comfortable place to sit on the floor, preferably somewhere you've never sat before. Maybe go outside if you rarely work in the open air – you might find it more stimulating.
5. Now that you are sitting somewhere fresh and new, be there for a minute – still – and then gently close your eyes. Keep them closed for a full minute or for as long as you feel you need to.
6. When you open your eyes, take a good long look around you and observe everything that is within your visual sphere. Do this for as long as you want.
7. Pick up a pen and simply let your hand flow over the paper with the first words that come into your head. They may be random words or they may even be whole sentences. DO NOT RE-READ OR CORRECT ANYTHING – this is important. Just write as much as you can without thinking too much.
8. If you wish, use a different colored pen for each new section, line, or subject/theme.
9. Don't stop until you have filled as much of the page as possible. Follow your instincts and use the intuitive guidance that will keep coming to move your hand forward. Use more paper if you get on a roll! This process of writing is called "Free Association".
10. Finally, look at the page or pages you have filled. TA-DA!

Congratulations ...
you are a writer.

Here is my effort – I wrote this while sitting in the corner of my spare room. My words and thoughts to begin with were based on observing what was in the far corner of the room.

Result 1:
Photo of me and my brothers as kids, we look so geeky! book on modern art, would love to take a nap, Kelly Klein's book *Pools*, the *Blue Planet* dvd series, a broken surfboard on the top of the cabinet, some woven baskets from Bali, a bunch of postcards, raggedy collection of straw hats, a butterfly covered notebook, that's the one I took to Arizona I think, being kind to oneself is such a task, free spirit, when am I going to get to those books all stacked up, wonder who lives in my old apartment now, higgledy-piggledy, hibiscus covered fabric cushion, the dog's tennis ball, my friend Chris's cattle dog "Zoe", It's hot today, wonder if I should go to the beach? Maybe just a swim. A small basketball, bathroom cabinet, long grass, vegetation, palm leaves, the mountain ridge view through the window, the passage of time is ...

Result 2:
I then began creating sentences using the keywords above as a starting point, linking these to some experiences from my childhood. I created a character, named her Zoe, and let her have her memories on my page.

Result 3:
I was on a roll now ... this is what came from my random words and thoughts.

continued...

Zoe dragged herself out of bed. Her body felt tired and heavy, from nothing in particular. Life, she thought, as she glimpsed and then avoided her own gaze in the bathroom mirror. Sighing at no one and for no reason in particular, she turned on the water and stepped into the shower. Once under she closed her eyes and let the water rain directly on her face, feeling every nerve end tingle in shock and pleasure. Colors flashed in front of her eyelids and she could just make out a weird image with moving fluorescent colors outlining a deeper purple-black outline. She strained to recognize the shape and realized it was her own artwork from school. This had been one of her favorite activities in art class as a small child, squeezing the paints into the crease of a page, which once opened made psychedelic butterflies.

Now she was seeing the whole classroom covered with them and her teacher, who looked like Cher, bending over her table smiling and then holding hers up to show the class. Her teacher's hair was dark and long and Zoe remembered having a crush on her. She was so gentle and kind, taking special care to encourage the precious artistic efforts of her charges. Zoe was so smitten that when her mother came to collect her from school she didn't even want to go home.

Suddenly it was years later and Zoe was playing King Ball in the playground. She had new black leather school shoes on and her short white socks contrasted sharply with her legs that were deep tan from the long summer at the beach. Her hair, sun-streaked brown from the sun, was falling out of its ponytail and strands were tucked carelessly behind one ear. Still undeveloped, her short pale blue checked uniform revealed nothing of a chest, yet she was as sensual as any tropical storm. Free in spirit with her huge blue eyes, lightly freckled nose and wide white smile, she ran and jumped, bouncing the ball off the chalk squares on the asphalt and beating all the boys, whose sideways glances she barely registered.

Then she remembered the long days that never seemed to end, picking wild blackberries with all the neighborhood kids. Poking around in the lantana and squealing with terror as someone shouted to watch out for the snake. Fear of snakes was a constant theme in those days and hardly a day passed without an encounter.

She recalled the willow trees by the creek, their long branches drooping lazily in the water, and the millions of amber leaves which fluttered into the rapids. She and her brothers would spend hours and sometimes days trying to dam the creek, up to their elbows in the red clay and peeling off the leeches which wriggled onto their ankles hoping for a blood fix, their shiny black bodies grotesquely puffy from other feedings. There were other hot days too, where she would lie on the blowup mattress in the pool, studying the turquoise water and watching the outline of the distant mountains through half-slits.

She remembered one summer in particular, the first time she ever sun-baked on her back, trying to get the front of her body brown, how she ended up with blisters on her stomach, sunburned for the first and only time in her life. She laid with her face up to the sun and saw patterns on the inside of her eyelids, opening them to occasionally squint at the clear sky through the holes in her straw hat, wondering if things would ever change. The cicadas droned incessantly, suddenly attaining a higher pitch, signaling a new wave of heat, and the air became even more still as the sweat ran rivers down her temples and her hair stuck to her neck. It was a test to see how long she could bear it, a little trick she played on herself. She would try to fool herself into thinking she was actually cold until she could stand it no longer, whereupon she would fling herself off the mattress into the cool water.

These were long days indeed, and although she wasn't even old enough to understand the concept of an endless summer, she knew that time could stand still. She was the river, clay, berry, leech, snake and mountain. She became the pool, cicada and the fierce heat. It was all her.

Phew! That was quite an outpouring. It even surprised me a bit. Through the use of the free association technique – I was able to tap into some old memories and re-craft them into a new person's experience and description. Some of these were vague memories I hadn't thought about in any detail for years. It became a very pleasurable exercise reliving a few long-forgotten moments. And while the actual piece of writing took about two hours, writing down the keywords took less than 20 seconds.

When crafting the final piece, for some reason it became a piece of creative writing, however it could just as easily been transformed into a journal or diary entry. If you look in each paragraph you can see many of the keywords have cropped up in the description of the character's memory or been the trigger for the next sequence.

Tune into your mind

What I hope the above exercise shows is a simple way to tune into your mind and free up some of the stuff you've literally filed away. Trust me, you may not even be aware of it yet, but there is a lot in there! Think of the joy of finding an old favorite T-shirt that hasn't seen the light of day for years stashed in the back of a drawer and then wearing it with a new skirt or jeans. It may be old but you can still make it seem new again ... Once it is retrieved from the file, all you have to do is write it down.

Whenever you feel yourself blocked in any way, then that is the perfect time to do the "Just For Fun" (free association) exercise. By keeping the emphasis on "Fun" the pressure to "Perform" is reduced in the mind. Ditto the colored pens and pencils. As with anything that you do over a long period of time, it must be mostly fun or you simply won't do it for long. In the same way, turning a creative activity into a serious challenge or a heavy task can kill the energy and the passion.

Keep it light and try not to be too "outcome-oriented" – just see what happens. Amazing results crop up this way. Let go and you can UN-BLOCK your Self wherever you are.

it's your life story

What the above exercise also shows is that "Your Life Story" is rich pickings for your writing endeavors.

You have lived a life, whatever your personal and family circumstances. You have met people, had conversations, gone to school, attended events and places, had family interactions, looked at the outside world, made many observations, and invariably formed opinions about it all.

You have most likely experienced any number of emotions: **joy, despair, confusion, heartbreak, happiness, contentment, frustration, rage** – these are all great things to consider and express.

You have done things on a daily basis that, whether you are aware of it yet or not, can be transformed into a piece of art. What you do every day may not seem like much, however even the smallest of experiences can be used in your writing. It's all juice! That is why it is so useful to keep a journal and to track what is going on in your life. And once you have the material, there will be no stopping you.

Loca

on, Location!

If you want to do it regularly and as a hobby, perhaps write in a different location to the desk or table that you might always sit at. Doing homework, university stuff or work you brought home from the office in the same spot as your writing can make a fun thing become another task on the long to-do list.

This is why I recommend taking yourself into a different environment to the one you normally do work in, to do the "Just For Fun" exercise. It proves that you can write anywhere, anytime and pretty much about anything at all.

I have written thousands of words in my journal while curled up like a pretzel on the narrow top bunk of an over-crowded train in India. I have written pages over a latte at airports, I have even written notes in the back of a yellow cab winging its way downtown on Fifth Avenue in Manhattan. The point is, once you get used to it, you can change the scenery when you are writing and you can write anywhere and everywhere.

No guts no glory!

The great thing about writing is that there is no limit to how much you can write if you have a strong enough desire. The bestselling romance novelist (and the aunt of Princess Diana) Barbara Cartland reportedly wrote a one hundred thousand-word novel per week for decades, continuing this cracking pace until she was well into her eighties. Her output was prolific and although the books may not have been to everyone's taste, she was obviously regularly compelled to write large quantities of words. **There is NO limit to what you can do!**

Another huge benefit of giving yourself the gift of writing is that you will have an activity for your entire life. And this also means: YOU NEED NEVER EVER BE BORED!

You will never be bored because anywhere you go, if you have a piece of paper and a pen that works, you can always write down your thoughts and observations. You can CRAFT something. You can CREATE something. You can DISCUSS something.

A short poem. Some dialogue. A descriptive paragraph. A letter. Random thoughts. The format is irrelevant to a writer with passion.

The real point is that by the act of writing, you will gain the ability to tap into your own subconscious and access layers of knowledge that may otherwise have been unreachable.

Writing can become your constant companion on your way through life. You can't be lonely when you talk to your journal – another great bonus.

Writing will show you your footprints – through the soft sand, the thick mud and the long grass of life.

Writing is your ultimate witness, showing where you've been and who you have become through incarnations and over time. In writing, **you allow your inner voice to be released.** You will start a conversation with your Self that will become stronger through the years.

A companion for life

You will no longer be
a stranger in paradise,
and nor will you be
a stranger to your Self.

2. Finding your voice

I can practically hear some girlo readers thinking, "But I don't have anything to say!" Well, you would if you could only find your voice and speak up. Finding your voice is an interesting thing. It can sometimes happen only when you have no one else to talk to!

What you may not even be conscious of – even if you feel you have nothing to say or to write – is the ongoing conversation in your head. Some of the most useful conversations happen when I am alone with my journal. This is usually (and logically) at its peak when I am traveling alone. It is also one of the main reasons why I always plan to write when I go on a trip. Two of the most important things I pack when I travel are my notebooks and a solid supply of pens. I often travel by myself, so these tools become my companions for the journey.

For a writer, this is where the nectar lies. It is the one conversation you can guarantee won't cease. Getting in touch with it and recording some of those observations and strange little dialogues that you have with your Self is a great resource for your writing.

To find your voice you have to do two things. Firstly, you must be in the right frame of mind to **LISTEN to your own conversation;** secondly, you must **put yourself in the right LOCATION** in order to let it all come out on the page!

Getting in touch

In the "Just For Fun" exercise, step 5 asks you to gently close your eyes. This is for two reasons.

One, when you close your eyes you automatically "go within". In closing your eyes and relaxing you take a rest from the outside world – looking at the backs of your eyelids (literally!) gives you a break from taking in the details of what surrounds you visually. Pulling the shutters down, so to speak, for a short period of time can be a mini-meditation. This is when you allow things to be however they are and you calmly stay in the moment. The Buddhists call this "being present".

Two, if you hold that action for a longer moment (and use it as a proper meditation), you can access a spaciousness that truly helps you to "see" once you do re-open your eyes. **Writing is about developing your awareness** and meditation does exactly that if done regularly.

Meditation allows you to just "be" and it allows your mind to go where it wants to. In quietness, the solution to a creative problem may float in. Or perhaps you will be still long enough to enable the clutter of daily life to recede. The creative thoughts you are hoping for might occur, instead. You never know what might come up: an idea for a small business, a novel, a course you want to take that might help you in your career, or even just an intuition that someone really needs to talk to you, which may lead somewhere else entirely.

In a previous girlosophy book I provide meditation instructions and I've included an updated version of it here in order to help those who may have not used this wonderful technique before.

"... to see the whole of anything, there must be – not the space that the word creates – the space of freedom. Only in freedom can you see the whole."
J. Krishmnamurti, from Freedom and Love in Action

Meditation:
YOUR QUICK STEP-BY-STEP GUIDE

To make an effective request of the Universe, your mind needs to be static-free — free, that is, from too many overlapping and conflicting thoughts. When you desire a clear response, you have to make a clear request. The same goes if you want to do something creative. As we know, a certain amount of clarity can help you accomplish major deeds when it comes to creative activities!

Thoughts are energy and any thought you are sending out amidst a whole bunch of other jumbled up thoughts has a greater chance of just getting lost in the maelstrom. Meditation is a heightened form of concentration which can be a very calming and powerful method of rewiring and refreshing your Self.

If you find yourself having too many negative thoughts, and/or if you find that you are often having feelings of being frustrated, meditation can be a great tool to re-balance your mind and rejuvenate your body. It can make sure your orientation is positive and not negative.

Meditation can enhance your focus on any goal and that includes any creative project you may need the inspiration to complete.

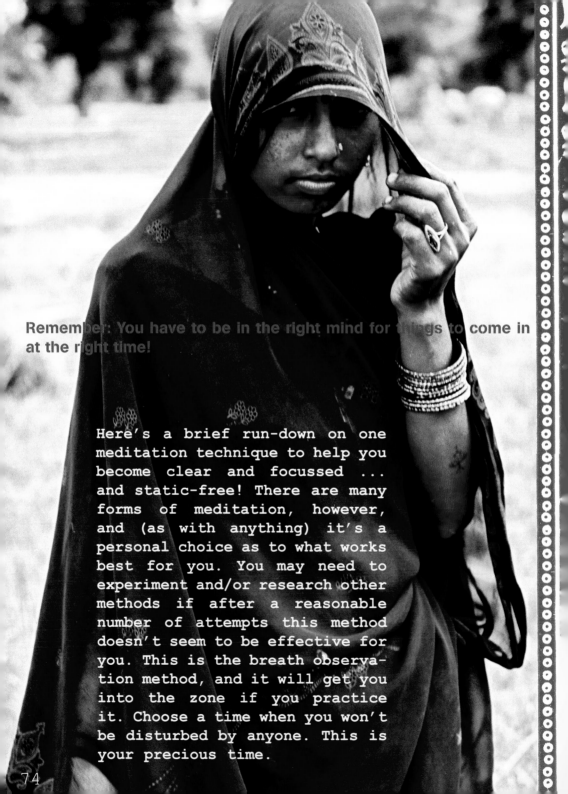

Remember: You have to be in the right mind for things to come in at the right time!

Here's a brief run-down on one meditation technique to help you become clear and focussed ... and static-free! There are many forms of meditation, however, and (as with anything) it's a personal choice as to what works best for you. You may need to experiment and/or research other methods if after a reasonable number of attempts this method doesn't seem to be effective for you. This is the breath observation method, and it will get you into the zone if you practice it. Choose a time when you won't be disturbed by anyone. This is your precious time.

Preparation:

First, take off your watch or set an alarm clock for a few minutes' time. Get comfortable by either sitting on your bed with your feet on the floor or sitting on the floor with your legs in a crossed position. If you prefer, rest your spine against the wall for support. You can even sit on a chair or, if you suffer from a bad back, lie on the floor. Whatever feels right for you.

Step 1. Breathe in through your nose with your mouth closed.

Step 2. Leave your eyes either half-open and focussed on one point in the room or, if you prefer, you can close them fully.

Step 3. Continue to breathe through your nose until you feel the breath go all the way to your stomach, and then breathe out the same way so you can feel a kind of "loop" pattern in your breathing.

Step 4. Don't follow any train of thought (I know this is hard but you have to allow them to fade out – letting go is the objective here). If any thoughts arise, let them fall away as you return your focus to your breath. The thoughts will continue to come but the trick is to learn to ignore them and to not attach to any in particular. They have no place for you right now because they are only serving to distract you from your mission of being peacefully static-free!

Step 5. If you find you have too many thoughts, practice running an affirmation over and over in your mind. For example: "I love my life. I am happy and contented. All is well in my world." You can change the meditation to suit your needs or your mood.

Step 6: Be still, don't fidget and really try to control any excess body movement. Focus. You can control your body! Do this for as long as you can. You can start with a few minutes and work up to longer periods. Do it first thing in the morning when you're fresh, and then again in the evening before you go to sleep.

BY BREATHING IN AND BREATHING OUT YOU WILL DISCOVER THAT MEDITATION IS ... PURE INSPIRATION.

The more, the

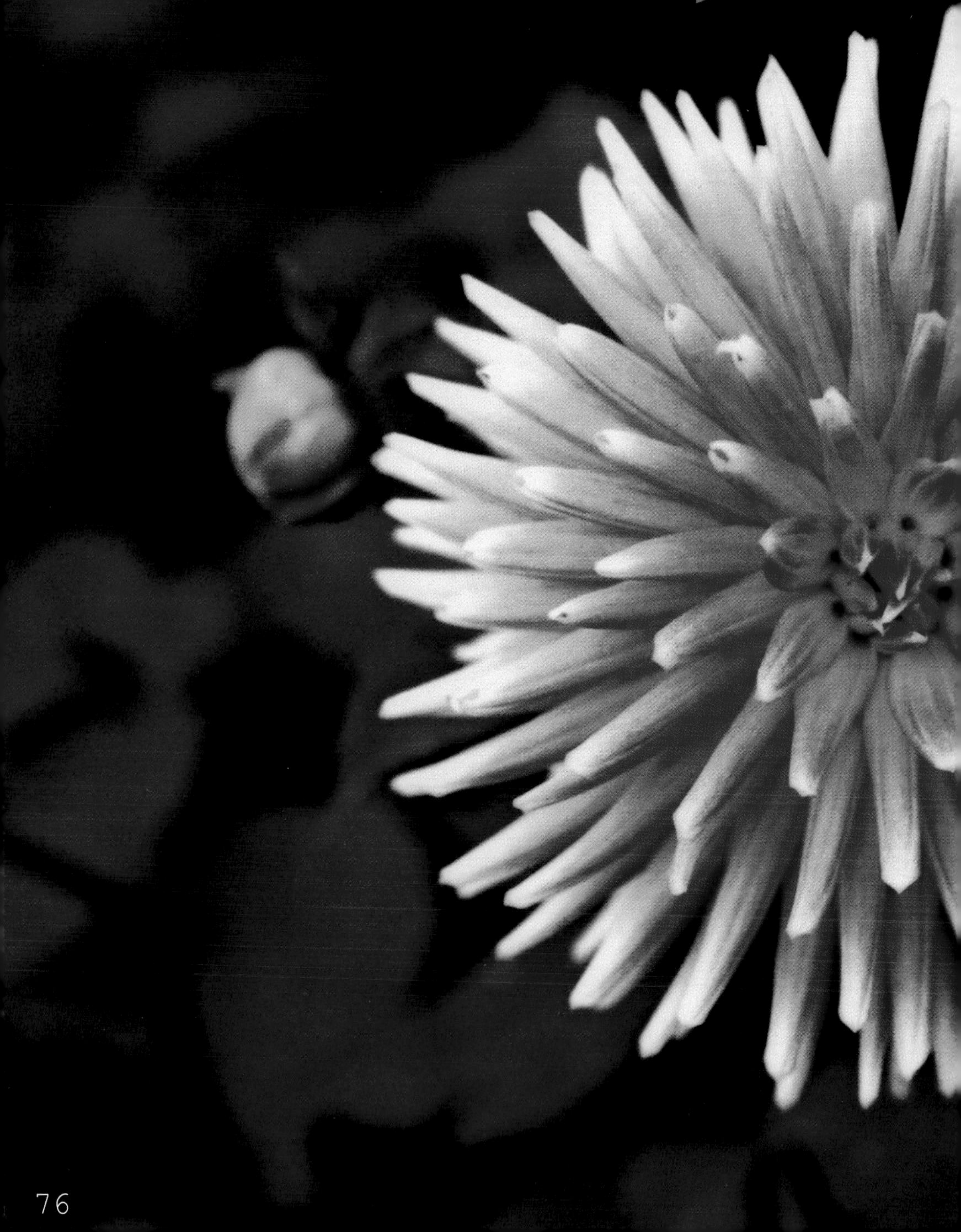

merrier!

The more you meditate, the greater the results will be – but you'll have to do a bit of work to really see and feel them. Meditation is just a great tool for life – irrespective of whether you do or don't wish to write. If nothing else, starting the day with a meditation session will really give you inner strength and an enhanced sense that things are possible. You will be more likely to think of the solution to something than to ruminate on the problem.

And it has been shown in extensive research that meditation improves immune function and helps cultivate a happier, more positive attitude in general. Not to mention, it will increase your chances of being creative during the day. That's why I like to do it early in the morning!

The ritual of writing

Meditation is one "ritual" you can use to prepare for writing. Over the years many colleagues and friends who write for a living have lifted the lid a little on what they do to get themselves ready for the screen or notebook. Some of the methods are prosaic: take a shower, two flat whites, mobile off, work flat-chat.

Some are more personal: A morning prayer to Saraswati, the Indian Goddess of Knowledge and the Arts; the burning of some incense or oils on a shrine next to the desk while working; playing specially selected music throughout the creative session (I recommend this!).

Some are practical: Wake up, drink endless cups of tea, do not leave the bed until at least 2000 words are written, then continue to write in pyjamas all day.

Some are cave-like: Lockdown in garage/home office with tray of food and a jug of filtered water. Do not emerge until dark. Write until spent.

Some people can't begin to write without a ritual. One writer I heard about lines all his pens and pencils in size order and works his way through them. I need to get outside in the fresh air first before sitting down to it. That usually works for me, then I can head to the studio knowing I've been "out there" in the world already.

In becoming a writer, you are finding your voice, but you should also create your own rituals that help you to get "in the zone". Find the spaces that work for you, the chair that is comfortable, the view that is soothing rather than distracting, the props you need (water, tissues, spare pens), the ambience that lends calmness not chaos (quiet soothing music) and, most crucially, the time to yourself to make it happen.

3. Themes & concepts

to work with and be jazzed by ...

In this section we get to some of the concepts that can help you and get you excited about writing. The aim here is to collect a bunch of themes, ideas and concepts to start your journaling life in the right direction.

In order to create something unique when writing, you sometimes need a bit of a shortcut. I have all sorts of tricks to get myself "in the mood" if I'm feeling a bit stale or lacking in inspiration. In this next exercise, much like the "Just For Fun" method, I give myself another little test. I make myself work with a word or sentence picked by me at random and then I just write from there.

I call this effective method "Shelf Life".

The "Shelf Life" Exercise

1. Go to your bookshelf or to the library at school or university.

2. Stand in front of the books, close your eyes and simply feel your way across their spines.

3. When your hand feels a bit warm or you get a sensation of heat under your palm (trust me it happens!) then stop your hand and pull out whatever book is underneath.

4. Open the book at any page.

5. Close your eyes and let your finger wander freely across the page until you feel like stopping.

6. Wherever you stop, let that word or phrase or sentence, whatever it is, be the subject of your writing.

7. Write about it. If possible, try and relate it to the day you are having or an experience you can recall.

Here is what I came up with doing this exercise. The book I landed on was called *Monsoon Diary*, a beautiful book by Indian writer Shoba Narayan. The words I stopped my finger at were on page 73:

"They came from all parts of Adyar and were bound by a consuming interest in cricket and little interest in me."

Shelf life

And in response, I wrote:

When you are a teenager it seems that life is always about boys and whether they like you – or not. In retrospect it is ridiculous how much agony that causes when you are growing up. I can remember the endless pain it caused, but it was purely due to me and my paranoia, as the boys in question were usually preoccupied with whatever they were doing. They certainly weren't deliberately trying to hurt me. So there was me, watching and hoping to be observed or noticed – and of course the real thing was that I needed to be approved of. In reality I was just part of the scenery, along with the neighborhood dogs and people going past and, well, just life in general.

Of course I now realize that the boys were in fact being the normal ones. I mean, they just continued on with their fun, skateboarding or bike riding or whatever they happened to be doing. Fair enough! It was me, apparently, who was "The Weirdo". It never occurred to me to think that the constant question, "Does he/Do they like me?" was actually MY problem!

Obsessions aside, one thing I learned, you can never compete with a group of boys and an activity they are wholly engaged in. And nor should you try!

I'm quite sure there is not a girl alive who hasn't at some point felt like chopped liver compared to a sporting match or some other exclusively male group gig. And I think it's something that stays with you for life, that feeling of being made to feel second. It can make you really resentful.

In reality, the solution is about being secure and the rather obvious thing of not needing approval to feel good about yourself. But that is so much harder when you are younger and everything seems to be so dramatic and extreme and angst-ridden!

My better – should I say "healthier"? – response to the problem at the time was that I became a keen skateboarder and simply joined in. I became part of the group activity instead of being a spectator. And when I took a major fall on the road where we used to practice, and sprained an ankle, quite apart from being laughed at and feeling embarrassed by it, I also remember getting all the attention I thought I deserved! But at least by that stage it was for the right reasons. So that was a lesson for life.

* * *

This riff could then (theoretically) flow or segue into many areas: 21st century relationships, women in sport, being self-sufficient, relating to guys, creating change, stories of other friends who may or may not be in a relationship, being independent, how to manage feeling good about yourself in different and challenging situations, etc.

The "Shelf life" exercise is a great warm-up technique to writing.

You may not always beat them at their own game, but you can certainly join them.

Your Personal Profile

In getting to know someone, we typically ask them questions. To get a broad sense of who they are – their profile and their character – we usually try and gain a basic overview of their life. If we are interested in developing a friendship, we go a bit deeper: we like to know where they were born and when, how many brothers and sisters they have, where they live, go to school or work, what they like to do, etc. We show we care about the essence of the person when we ask these questions because it goes beyond a superficial interest.

Getting to Know ... YOU

Getting to know your Self is probably not too dissimilar. Of course, many of the basic facts you will already know, but what if you dug a little deeper with the aim of discovering other things so you consciously know your Self even more?

In this section the focus is on creating a Personal Profile that can be used as a platform from which you can spring from to write more openly.

As we have been discussing, putting things on paper is quite an intimate, difficult process. It may even be more difficult if it forces you to think about things that you may not have fully or properly considered – or even wanted to think about. But if intimacy with your Self is the key to developing intimacy with others, then writing down some of the details about yourself can be very positive and therapeutic.

I should mention that initially this process may seem a little self-absorbed – not to mention somewhat self-indulgent – but I recommend it as an exercise to "warm up". For many people, creating a Personal Profile is the first step towards Self-knowledge and it can unlock memories, feelings and emotions that have been long suppressed or just forgotten.

A spirit of individual truth-telling and bare honesty then guides your creative tasks.

This path can lead to extraordinary revelations. There may also be a sense of "aliveness" in the writer as the creative channels clear – old stuff is "outed" and new energy rushes through.

A checklist for old time's sake!

The list of questions and subjects below is fairly free ranging and limited in scope only by the imagination of the profiler. As you will see, the questions run from the extremely basic to the far more complex.

You can add to the list, delete some items or re-arrange the order as you prefer – what I've provided is only a basic blueprint. If anything it should be personalized by you to be truly effective. (Note to would-be fiction writers: this is a seriously useful technique for understanding characters you may be working on and for writing backstories or subplots.)

In addition, your list may change over time, so it can be a fun thing to revisit. What was important to you in the past may have changed and you can update your list to reflect current concerns, new personal preferences and discoveries.

Note to girlo readers: At the end of doing this exercise, you may be quite surprised to see who you are on the page! Perhaps you might like to begin your journal with your Personal Profile answers. In this way you can kick start your book of creativity with a bang!

Above all, creating your Personal Profile is just another way to help you think outside the usual box and generate creative thinking. There is no "one way" to write. There is no correct answer to your internal questions except as your heart tells you. Be fresh and daring in your answers. May you receive many happy returns ...

YOUR PERSONAL PROFILE

The facts about me
My past
My future
My present
My destiny is ...

Your Personal Profile

THE FACTS ABOUT ME

My full name is …
I was born on … (day / month / date)
I was born at … (time) in … (town, state, country)
I am a … citizen and this makes me feel …
My star sign is …
My parents are …
I have … siblings (if you have them!)
I am currently at … school / university / college or
I currently work at …
What I like about my school studies / job is …
What I dislike about my school studies / job is …
I am saving up for … because …
My home is in … (place) and I have lived here for … (years)
My friends are … (names and descriptions)
I love people who … (take risks / tell funny stories, etc.)
My favorite activity / activities include …
and I love to do this … because …
My favorite color is … because it reminds me of …
I love to say … and my most over-used saying is probably …
My favorite meal involves … and my favorite snack food is …
I consider myself to be … (healthy / unhealthy) and fitness …
is / is not important to me. This is due to factors such as …
Changes to my lifestyle I would like to make include …
I am … (clean / messy / organized / chaotic)
I lose / don't lose things
I don't need to change anything about my life or lifestyle because …
The person who supports me the most is …
and in my life they have helped me to …
The best time of the day to me is … because …
I like … (sunrise / sunset) the most because …
I need to have … every day
I hope to hear … (music / bands / a phrase / poetry / a speaker)
I want to see … (films / shows / flowers / nature, etc.)
I am frightened by … (snakes / cockroaches / bills / the dark)
and this makes me …
My favorite movie of all time is …

My greatest inspiration is ...
My all-time role model is ... because ...
I would like to be like ... because ...
I respect ... because (he / she) ...

MY PAST

When I was little I remember that ...
I felt ... (happy / sad or other emotions)
My childhood was generally ... (positive / negative, etc.)
and this is because ...
My family is ... (amazing / crazy / sad / wonderful / split up, etc.)
and they are ... because ...
The good times I remember were ...
The hard times I can remember include ...
I find / always found school to be ... (easy / difficult / fun, etc.)
and this is because ...
The best teacher I ever had was ... because he / she ...
and that made me realize that ...
The worst teacher I ever had was ... because he / she ...
and that made me realize that ...
The music I like to listen to is ... because it sounds like ...
and it makes me feel ...
I grew up thinking that ...
I changed when ...
The first concert event I ever went to was ... (band / event)
at the ... (place) and I went with ...
I found the experience of being in a large crowd to be ...
(description)
The best holiday I ever had was ... when I went to ...
with ...and we ... (description)
The best thing anyone has ever said to me is ...
The worst thing anyone has ever said to me is ...
What no one has ever told me is ...
My first crush on someone was ... because ...
and it happened when ... because ...
The first time someone had a crush on me was ...
and it felt ... because ... and it turned out to be ... because ...
The most fun I ever had was when ... and ... because ...

In the past I have been hurt by … when … because …
In the past I have hurt … when I … because … and I feel … about it
My most successful day was when I …
The first time someone had a crush on me was … and it felt …
because … and it turned out to be … because …
In the past I have been hurt by … when … because …
In the past I have hurt … when I … because … and I feel … about it
My most successful day was when I …
I received recognition when I
(graduated / won a prize / got a job / moved out, etc.)
I am proud that I …
I look back at my life and I feel that … because …
The greatest lesson I learned was … and I learned it when …
The wisest thing anyone ever told me was … and it helped me to …
The first time I was scared was when …
The last time I went out was …
The highlight of my school years was …
The greatest risk I ever took was when I …
The best result I ever got was when I …
The worst thing that ever happened to me was …
The peak experience of my teen years was …
The craziest thing that ever happened to me was …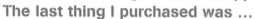
The funniest thing that ever happened to me was …
The last thing I purchased was …

MY FUTURE

In my teens I hope to achieve …
In my twenties I hope to achieve …
In my thirties I hope to achieve …
In my forties I hope to achieve …
When I am older I would like to be …
When I am older I would like to do …
I would love to travel to … because …
I think marriage is …
I would like / would not like
(to be married / to be single / living in a share house / living alone)
I think children are … (awesome / a great thing / a burden / un-
necessary, etc.) … and I would like to / not like to … have children
/ adopt children
I think having a career is … and I would like to be …
so that I can … with my life
The goals I have include …
I am looking forward to …
I am worried about …
I am confident that …
I feel uncertain of …
I know for sure that …

MY PRESENT

I love … I believe … I am happy when … I feel uncomfortable if …
I need to … I think that … I have an instinct about … My dreams
are … It is important to … I am upset about … I find these things
funny / hilarious … I find these things sad / devastating … I am
joyful about … I am waiting until … before I … I am in love with
… because … I am grieving about … I am concerned that … I am
conflicted by … I am confused that … I am angry that … I am sorry
about … I am interested in … I am thrilled by … I would like to be
… I would like to have … I would like to change … I am scared that
… My most secret desire is … I like it when … I dislike it when … I
love how … I hate it when … I have the strangest feeling that … I
find … beautiful and it … I think that I cannot … I find … ugly as it
… I think … is silly because … I think … is tragic because … What
no one realizes about me is … I see … I find it easy to … I find it
hard to … I am at my best when … I can do … I am tired of … I am
excited by … I hope that … My destiny is …

Chakra connections:

For those girlo readers who came a bit late to class, I will include a bit of a quickie overview of the Chakra system, so you're up to speed when you read this next section.

What is the Chakra System?

As a girlosopher you have a physical life, a mental life and a spiritual life. And as you know, you exist on both the material and spiritual planes at the same time. The connections between these two dimensions are your Chakras – what I call energy "hotspots" located in your body – and the way in which you are "plugged in" to the universal energy flow. Combined they form a system: the Chakra System.

What's the point of the Chakra System?

Chakras are the key to healing any dis-ease or lack of ease existing between your mind, body and spirit. You can feel when things are not flowing easily in your life and normally this will be associated with an illness in the region of the Chakra you need to work on. So as you can see, it's pretty crucial to understand and get in touch with each of them – they can really help you on your journey towards wholeness as a person.

Be your own Oracle!

Where do I find each of the Chakras?

Traditionally, there are seven Chakras. Each Chakra is associated with a particular region of the body with its own purpose and each is a source for healing therapy. Here's the brief list:

- **Crown Chakra (top of the head in the center)**
- **Third Eye Chakra (between your eyebrows)**
- **Throat Chakra (center and front of your neck region)**
- **Heart Chakra (center of your chest)**
- **Solar Plexus or Power Chakra (located under your rib cage)**
- **Lower Abdomen or Sacral Chakra (just below your navel)**
- **Base Chakra (located directly underneath the base of your pelvis).**

(For those girlo readers who would like more detail, please refer to girlosophy – *The Oracle* and girlosophy and girlosophy – *The Breakup Survival Kit*.)

Chakra connections:

Now you are up to speed, consider how the Chakras are associated with many emotions and thoughts, and how they have powerful effects when it comes to your creativity. When the Chakras are in flow, you are in flow. If one or two are out of whack, you'll be amazed at the difference it can make to your output. If you are unwell in any area, this means the Chakra is not balanced, and so the energy is not flowing freely.

Types of emotions and illness (dis-ease) are associated with each Chakra.
In a positive sense, these can form the basis for your journal entries. You can see your illness as an opportunity for growth.
If, say, you are struggling with a sore throat, then perhaps it is the fifth Chakra you should focus on in your writing.

Ask yourself:
What do I want to say?
How should I best say what I feel?
Am I speaking my truth?
What am I NOT saying?
Who do I need to say something to?

Mapping you way to wellness can put you back in control. You can heal your Self if you are prepared to be
honest with yourself.

Below is the list of themes and words associated with
each Chakra. If you are not sure what Chakra to work
with, it may be a helpful exercise to try and write a
paragraph on each of the themes.

If that seems too much, then perhaps you could try to
write a line on each of the words associated with each
theme. The themes or words that are more of a struggle
to write about may be an indication of areas where you
have unresolved issues.

Use this knowledge as the cue to go deeper.

Pages of joy!

CROWN CHAKRA – DESTINY

Keywords:

- Destiny
- The Universe
- Consciousness
- Connection
- Direction
- Personal purpose
- Unity
- Wholistic
- The greater good

THIRD EYE CHAKRA – CROSSROADS

Keywords:

- Decisions
- Turning points
- Path
- Perception
- Psychic qualities
- Dreams
- Concentration
- Focus
- Enlightenment
- Intuition
- Awareness

THROAT CHAKRA – TRUTH

Keywords:

- Truth
- Communication
- Expression
- Silence
- Dialogue
- Emotions
  (spoken vs unspoken)
- Understanding
- Honesty
- Closure

HEART CHAKRA – LOVE

Keywords:

- Love
- Heart
- Intuition
- Mediation
- Compassion
- Surrender
- Process
- Unconditionally
- Passion
- Bliss
- Freedom

SOLAR PLEXUS / POWER CHAKRA – OMENS

Keywords:

- Omens
- Signs
- Free will
- Personal power
- Emotions
- Desire
- Intuition
- Flow
- Harmony
- Trust

LOWER ABDOMEN / SACRAL CHAKRA – KARMA

Keywords:

- Actions
- Reactions
- Creative impulses
- Sexuality
- Relationships
- Beauty
- Physicality vs spirituality
- Expression of needs
- Expression of desires

BASE CHAKRA – SURVIVAL

Keywords:

- Life issues / practical stuff
- Fear vs faith
- Physicality
- Instinct
- Doing vs being
- Ambition
- Formation of Self
- Survival
- Personality
- Protection of Self
- Success vs failure

The Chakras can help you focus your writing efforts. Writing allows you to express the things you may have difficulty saying, even to yourself. You will find that the answers to an issue you may be dealing with will become clearer. In the process you can heal yourself or, at the very least, write your way to a newfound balance. You can be your own Oracle! This is real Self-help.

103

our family stories are ...

We will all take our stories with us after we are gone.
We owe it to them and to ourselves to write them down, preserve
them and pass them on.

who you are

As you probably know, it is useful to get material from your own life experiences and adapt it to new "playing conditions". In this section I would like you to consider your family's stories. These may have been passed down from your great grandmother, perhaps, to your mother or father, and they are frequently worthy of being the plot of any film you might go and see. These stories tell you about your family and your roots, they are the story of your family tree.

Your ancestry is why you are who you are. The stories that your older relatives may have from 1960s protest marches, to wars or the Great Depression, or of emigrating from another country, are all important things to know. These details help you to join the dots on your own background and help you to understand your own family better, as well as your Self.

Not only are they fascinating and interesting stories, writing them down will lend an authenticity and a beating heart to your journal writing. **This is the cultural spirit.**

Talk to family members about their experiences. They may even have memories about you from when you were too young to recall. They will take these stories to their grave if you don't ask about them.

The global girlosopher

I have been contacted by many girlo readers asking me if I can recommend a trip they can take. This is always really difficult for me to answer - there are so many places to go in the world!

One of the most positive ways for those girlo readers who really want to have an experience and travel is to be a volunteer at a non-government organization (NGO) or an aid agency or some other group that relies on people who have time to give to others in need. There are projects all over the world - many people need help. There are many groups and many projects, it's more a case of where you want to go and how you want to spend your time while you are away.

Volunteering is also a fantastic opportunity to keep a journal of your experiences. Maybe you could come back and help set up a web-site to raise awareness or just publish an article in your local paper. You could end up writing a book. **All you need is a ticket and the desire to get out there.**

4. Trying a new format on for size . . .

Occasionally your journal may feel like "Groundhog Day". It's all a bit flat, so a new format to get jazzed about writing again may be just the ticket. Changing the format of your writing can put the zing back in your scribbles. **Here are some different ways of communicating to yourself and others that might just be what you are looking for.**

Real Girls write ... letters!

There is nothing more enjoyable than writing one, unless perhaps it is receiving a letter from someone else. Good old-fashioned letters are sadly fading into the distance as email and weblogs – "blogs" – take over. As genteel an activity as serving afternoon tea, formal letter writing as a means of communication is a dying art form.

Personal letters are usually (or should be) handwritten and are often intimate in content. They are designed to be revelatory – the beauty and the difference between sending a handwritten note or sending an electronic one.

Writing and then actually posting a letter to someone takes effort and commitment: you have to select the card or stationery, write the message (or story or life update) in your own script, finish it, furnish the correct address details, add stamps and get to a post box or post office to send it. Phew! But it's worth the effort. Take a look at this one.

My sweet Katai,
I have gone north. Come to Chiang Saen with my friend who brings this. I will meet you there Saturday at Tang Guest House.
Be careful. Always remember what we say: Eyes open, mouth shut.
And that I love you.
... Your mad dog.
Charles Nicholl, from Borderlines: A Journey in Thailand and Burma

Letters are impossibly romantic. The mass-circulated email has taken much of the intimacy and one-on-one nature out of correspondence. It can leave us feeling like we are one of a crowd at all times. There is no doubt that emails are a very handy way to stay in touch with people (and at least you're writing something!), however, as a form of communication, handwriting a letter is a completely different energy.

That's why I love letters and postcards. They can't go to too many people. They are special, personal missives, often from a far-flung location, telling the people we care about that we are thinking of them, even though we are at a distance.

Dear San & Mike,
Weather here, wish you were perfect!
Nobody knows the truffles I've seen ...
Postcard from a family friend traveling in France

I think postcards are the most wonderful invention. I love sending them (the gorgeous, the weird, and the tacky) and I love receiving them (the witty, the wild, the nostalgic) even more. I get such a kick to think someone has sat down at the local cafe in Legian or somewhere else exotic and taken a moment to write to me. I can practically smell the frangipani and incense through the writing.

One of the most delightful series of books is Nick Bantock's *Griffin & Sabine*. They are beautifully designed. As you read them you are reading the correspondence between two people who have never met. The books actually have postcards and letters included within the pages. You simply take a letter from the envelope and delve into the characters' intimate and growing relationship. I recommend all of them for inspiration (see Girlo Library for details).

"Long before I wrote my first song, words formed as poems in my journals; and poetry drives my song writing today."
Jewel, from A Night Without Armor

For anyone who hasn't yet had the experience, the discovery of the world of poetry is joyful. Poems are the simplest to read yet are often the most difficult things to write well. Reading really good poetry is a bit like visiting the Taj Mahal – the inherent balance and perfection of the form renders you instantly at peace and leaves you wanting more.

There are many types of poetry. Obviously Shakespeare left a formidable legacy of both poetry and plays, but the Great Bard's style may not flow with yours! Ted Hughes, John Donne, Sylvia Plath, T.S. Eliot, et al. are of course the mainstay poets of secondary schools the world over. But some of our greatest contemporary musicians are poets as well – think Bob Dylan, Joan Baez, Jewel, Neil Finn, Sting, Nick Cave, P.J. Harvey, Mazzy Star, among others. Some have even published books of poetry (see Jewel quote on left).

Making a foray into poetry via Japan rather than medieval England, may provide ongoing inspiration for girlo writers. Enter the "Haiku".

A Haiku is a classic, traditional form of Japanese poem.

In the Haiku, the parameters are fixed. It is a standard, one-size-fits-all poem which, on the one hand, forces you to be selective in your choices but, on the other, curiously allows for the most creative response. With its spare form it is surely the most elegant of poems.

The Haiku relies on three lines containing 17 syllables. There is a fixed number of beats per line – 5, 7, 5 – to make the 17 syllables. An example, by one of the masters of the form, Akutagawa Ryunosuke (1892-1927), is:

Sick and feverish   (5 syllables)
Glimpse of cherry blossoms   (7)
Still shivering   (5)

Or this one by Murakami Kijo (1865-1938):
The moment two bubbles
are united, they both vanish
A lotus blooms

You could create these all day!

But poetry is a world unto itself. Some people prefer to write theirs as rhyming prose, some simply like the more random, spare approach. As an example of the latter approach, Dorothy Porter's poetry is both challenging and inspiring.

Of course, if you have it within you to write poetry as beautiful as that of the 14th century Sufi poet Rumi, then you are truly blessed with a gift. For the rest of us who aspire to write poetry without quite the same talent or dedication, the following holds true: good poems are rare and bad poetry is everywhere.

In poetry, the general rule is that there aren't many rules. You can pretty much do your own thing – especially in the confines of your own journal. Be brave and above all, enjoy the process.

In your light, I learn how to love.
In your beauty, how to make poems.

You dance inside my chest,
where no one sees you,

but sometimes I do,
and that sight becomes this art.

Rumi, from The Essential Rumi (translated by Coleman Barks with John Moyne)

Essays are an exulted form of writing. Not to be confused with the dreaded school or university essay, an essay – a short literary composition – is actually a magical creation! Put simply, an essay is a meditation on a subject.

The essay is often overlooked as a creative piece. Books are sometimes created as a collection of essays. Journalists or columnists in newspapers write essays, sometimes daily or weekly, as it's their job! So it's a useful and comprehensive way of approaching and rounding out a subject.

If you aspire to variety within your journal or diary and if you want to challenge yourself creatively then an essay might just fit the bill. Pick a subject and let it rip.

For an excellent example of an essay, refer to Ashley Willcox's moving story "Reality in Recovery" in the "Real Girls Write!" section.

Journals and diaries

I have always written journals or diaries throughout my life. Whether in the form of sticker and pop star-covered school exercise books, key-lock diaries, scrapbooks, spiral notebooks, company letterheads, hotel phone pads, blank journals or even the odd Post-it note version, recording my world has been a necessary and ongoing activity for me.

Even if through certain periods I was more sporadic than regular in keeping up to date with my journals, I have certainly filled my share of blank pages (which is not to say it was always quality stuff!). But it doesn't matter. The point is in the exercise. Sometimes my journals have been absolutely hilarious to look back on and re-read (for example, I'm thinking of my school stuff here) and sometimes amazing (my various travel experiences). Far more often they were plain embarrassing (those that usually had something to do with a crush or unrequited love).

Several journals of mine have met an early and necessary end in a nearby bin or raging winter fireplace. At least one met the shredder at work. (Clearly, I wasn't so non-judgmental about any of those!)

Some journals I have kept because they are crucial reminders of a passage of time that has slipped into dim memory. Those that have survived are mostly from my traveling experiences. Yet no matter what became of my journals over time or how they now seem to me in retrospect, they have all served their purpose - and mine.

Dream Journals

Dreams are gorgeous, strange and mysterious things! Sometimes we can remember a particular dream clearly, but often it's a vague recollection, with snippets of conversation and fragments of imagery. Dreams may stay with you forever – they can be profound experiences (such as nightmares!) or they can just be a particular moment that was so vivid, it doesn't leave you when you wake in the morning. Whether you are aware of it or not, your dreaming takes place every night while you sleep.

One of the earliest pioneers of dream psychology was Carl Jung. He was convinced that in our minds lies the great subconscious connecting us with the Universe. Jung's lifework was based on the notion that all the images and scenes occurring in our dreams are meaningful and often highly symbolic. He developed a language to talk about dreams. "Archetypes" meant the universal symbols that could be applied to dreams and experiences. Jung firmly believed this to be the key to unlocking the subconscious mind in order to access the universal wisdom. To Jung, the subconscious mind was much like a giant code we are meant to crack.

Enter the Dream Journal! The idea of keeping a journal of your dreams is that on waking (while the memory of the dream is still fresh) you reach for a journal and record everything that you can remember, in as much detail as possible.

Keep a pen and a notepad on the bedside table. You may be inspired to write it during the night if your dream is so particularly vivid that it wakens you.

Maybe you could even divide your journal into a Day/ Night Journal. On the Day side write what is going on in your conscious life, on the other write down your dreams as they occur – your subconscious life. Are there any parallels or any recurring themes in each or in both? Do you have one dream that appears regularly?

Compare the two sides of the journal. What's going on for you? Are you dreaming of Tom Cruise? Apparently more people report dreaming of Tom Cruise than any other celebrity. Or are you dreaming of Madonna? Pop Queen Madge is so dreamed about there is even a book on the subject: *I Dream of Madonna*.

Do you dream in color or black and white? Maybe the vision of your dreams can become the subject of a drawing or painting or some other form of art. Maybe it's a case of déjà vu – you've been there before and it's all seemed like a dream you had a long time ago. Whatever it is, write it all down!

Affirmations Journals

Affirmations are life changing. In the best sense, affirmations are the sort of statement that say, "I AM ... ", and "I CAN ...". They can assist in areas of your life where you may have difficulties, or even where you lack experience, just through helping you to think positive and to have a go! Affirmations can even remove old habits, replacing them with new more helpful and healthy ones.

Affirmations are the kind of conversations that your negative mind needs when it just gets too, well, negative. They may encourage you to be more thoughtful, determined or perhaps just confident to take a risk.

An affirmations journal may be really useful for those girlo readers who would like to incorporate healthy thinking into their day. Imagine writing down hundreds of positive statements while you're waiting for the train or the bus, giving yourself a good pep talk? This is theme journaling at its best!

Below are some very cool and helpful affirmations just to get you going. While these are certainly general ones, I should mention that the best affirmations are the ones you write for yourself. When it's written in your words, the specific things you need to hear or that relate to your life somehow – and for some reason – resonate strongly.

If you don't wish to dedicate a specific journal to your affirmations, you may instead wish to use a daily affirmation in your regular writing journal.

It's a positive way to start and end the day.

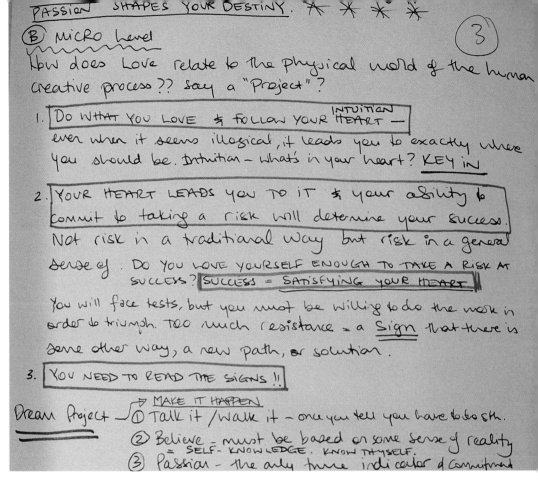

PASSION SHAPES YOUR DESTINY. ✳ ✳ ✳ ✳

B) MICRO Level ③

How does Love relate to the physical world of the human creative process?? Say a "Project"?

1. Do WHAT YOU LOVE & FOLLOW YOUR HEART — INTUITION
even when it seems illogical, it leads you to exactly where you should be. Intuition — what's in your heart? KEY IN

2. YOUR HEART LEADS YOU TO IT & your ability to commit to taking a risk will determine your success. Not risk in a traditional way but risk in a general sense of : DO YOU LOVE YOURSELF ENOUGH TO TAKE A RISK AT SUCCESS? SUCCESS = SATISFYING YOUR HEART

You will face tests, but you must be willing to do the work in order to triumph. Too much resistance = a Sign that there is some other way, a new path, or solution.

3. YOU NEED TO READ THE SIGNS !!

Dream Project — MAKE IT HAPPEN
① Talk it / Walk it — once you tell you have to do sth.
② Believe — must be based on some sense of reality = SELF- KNOWLEDGE. KNOW THYSELF.
③ Passion — the only true indicator of commitment

I am powerful and I use this power for the highest good.
I am peaceful. I follow my bliss!
I am kind.
I love and am loved in return.
I know myself. I am gentle with myself.
I am connected to all that I see.
I can do anything.
I am successful in life.
I act for the highest benefit of all concerned.
I am safe.
I am strong.
I believe in myself.
I am confident in my own ability.
I am a beautiful person.
I am healthy and happy.
My destiny is perfect for me.

Scrapbooks

I love all sorts of art. Whether it is fine art or not it can still stimulate me in some way. I always collect postcards, stickers, pull tear sheets from magazines and keep cards I receive. I am inspired by animation and I am also obsessed with pinboards. My fridge has even been known to be filled with overlapping pictures, photos, Post-it notes, emails, cards, mementos - you name it - it's certainly been a massive collage at times!

I am a visual person, and notwithstanding my love of words, books and reading, my world invariably consists of an over-abundance of visual references. The imagery that appeals to me may be beautiful, weird, or just interesting. If I respond to it on some level then it has done its job and often it is retained. Sometimes images are filed away for years until I need inspiration. They might then be filched out and, more often than not, just hang around the studio for a while.

Put it this way: it definitely works.
And the scrapbook/pinboard/journal "combo" is pretty much how the first girlosophy book girlosophy - *A Soul Survival Kit* came to be. There is the proof of the method to my madness!

To me a scrapbook is simply a mobile collage. Merging a journal and a visual diary to create a scrapbook provides you with a canvas for life.

The happy result of such obsessive collecting(!) is that not only do the visual imagery and the accompanying words or theme/s create something intensely personal but also (and this is always my hope) eventually something universal.

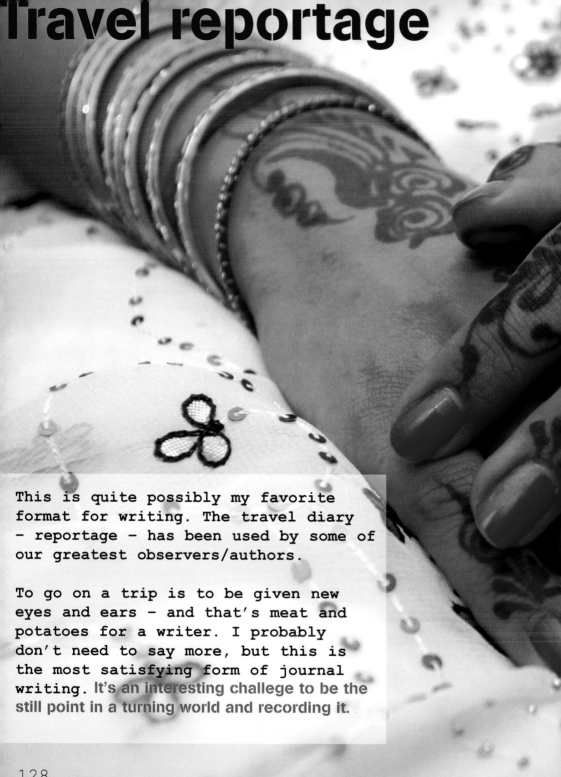

Travel reportage

This is quite possibly my favorite format for writing. The travel diary – reportage – has been used by some of our greatest observers/authors.

To go on a trip is to be given new eyes and ears – and that's meat and potatoes for a writer. I probably don't need to say more, but this is the most satisfying form of journal writing. It's an interesting challege to be the still point in a turning world and recording it.

There are many words of wisdom that have been spoken and written by well-known people throughout history. Some quotes have become so legendary that they are merely part of our language. Winston Churchill's "Never give up, never ever give up" is one such oft-quoted line. As it is said, if you want to be one of the greats, you have to read them first!

Quotes from history to the present day are worth collecting in your journal. Just hearing them can provide inspiration and uplift you energetically in a crucial moment. Writing down quotes and inspiring passages from books can be an invaluable resource for future projects.

Below is a selection of quotes that may serve to inspire you. They have certainly inspired me.

inspirations

"I'm just trying to talk about loves, relationships, life, death, pride, sex, existing ... Just all the things around us that make a difference."
Neneh Cherry, singer, songwriter, activist

"Life shrinks or expands according to one's courage."
Anais Nin, writer, philosopher

"To be successful, the first thing to do is to fall in love with your work."
Sister Mary Lauretta, Roman Catholic nun

"You must do the thing you think you cannot do."
Eleanor Roosevelt, American stateswoman

"And the trouble is, if you don't risk anything, you risk even more."
Erica Jong, author and writer, feminist

"Everything on the earth has a purpose, every disease and herb to cure it, and every person a mission. This is the Indian theory of existence."
Mourning Dove [Christine Quintasket] (1888–1936), Native American Indian

"If your inspiration, say for writing, comes out of pain, and you find yourself in a position where you don't feel that pain, you may not be able to write. But if the gift comes out of you, you can't help but grow with it."
Rickie Lee Jones, singer/songwriter

"Never give a diamond to a monkey."
Katai in Borderlines: A Journey in Thailand and Burma by Charles Nicholl

"One must live in the present tense, but I have always lived in the present tensely."
Bette Davis, actor, legend

"Most important of all, however, is 'to tame this mind of ours'. If we can realize the true nature of our own mind, then this is the whole point of both the teaching and our entire existence."
Sogyal Rinpoche, Tibetan Master, from Natural Great Peace

"We don't see things as they are, we see them as we are."
Anais Nin, writer, philosopher

"There are no ordinary people."
C.S. Lewis, from The Weight of Glory

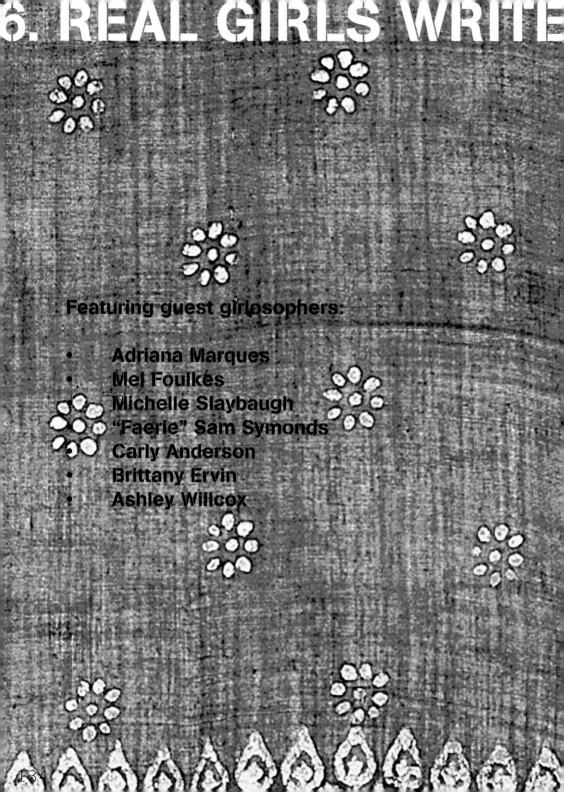

6. REAL GIRLS WRITE

Featuring guest girlosophers:

- Adriana Marques
- Mel Foulkes
- Michelle Slaybaugh
- "Faerie" Sam Symonds
- Carly Anderson
- Brittany Ervin
- Ashley Willcox

So let's start ... listening to Flake, Jack Johnson.

I will tell my story from the beginning ... Then you can see who I am, and understand better my journal. In the past three months, I felt I was part of a movie, and even thought about writing a book. You will understand why.

I'm 28 years old, from São Paulo, southeast of Brazil. I'm an adopted child. I've never met my biological parents. I can say I am very lucky because my family is definitely great!!! I have 2 brothers Claudio and Wilson, and a sister called Eliana. My sister was 19 when I arrived. What a difference! When I was six, I was an aunt already!!! **I had a memorable childhood**. I grew up with my cousins Vivian and Liliane, they are like my sisters. Vivian got married last June, but I couldn't attend the wedding because I was in Australia. Lili's wedding will be in 2 weeks, we are sooo excited about it! Tomorrow I will see my dress for the celebration ...

I started to work after high school when I was 17 in a doctor's office, as a personal assistant, I took care of the clinic as if it was mine. This doctor is very important in Brazil and I had the chance to meet heaps of interesting people from the arts, literature, and TV worlds. I also had a reasonable wage, I could afford to pay my university fees, take extra courses like English, and pay for a car and things I needed. My family is not rich; after starting work I couldn't depend on them anymore.

I graduated in Social Communication in 1999. I like my profession, but now mainly after traveling. I think I chose it very early, but it is still relevant to my personality. I realized I like to work with people spreading information not only here in my country but with all cultures.

In my last year at university, we decided to do our graduating work about an NGO, an organization responsible in raising funds and taking care of people with AIDS. I was responsible for the Communication Plan. I also got an internship in a Communication Agency in my holidays at the office.

After getting my degree, I went to an intensive English course, one of my passions! I ended up being invited to be a teacher in the school. I taught for about 6 months before deciding to go abroad. I needed to do it for myself, personal issues, apart from improving and getting out into the so-called university of life.

I chose Australia because it is an exotic country, on the other side of the world. The ticket was more expensive, but the cost of life was cheaper for me if compared to the USA and London. I was also excited about the modern culture and similar weather. I found out that a friend of mine Oscar wanted to go as well, so we started to plan together.

I did everything for my dream: I quit my job, sold my car and sorted out all the visa stuff which is very hard for Brazilians. Not impossible though ... We had to present lots of documents and prove we had enough money to survive each month we intended to live there. I went nuts, but everything went fine and I embarked to the "land of plenty".

I didn't live with my friend, I chose to stay with an Aussie family instead. I had to be involved in this new culture and not just speak Portuguese which would have been easier. I was scared and excited at the beginning, but I wasn't that comfortable with them. But to my surprise, they were more than I expected, and I learned a lot. I can now say they are like my second family! The couple were called Bob and Mary-Anne, and their 5-year-old, Elle, "The Princess", as I used to call her.

In Brisbane I studied at an International College and worked in a few jobs that school provided to us such as cleaning and working as a waitress. I learned a lot from these experiences about finding solutions to problems when you are far away from your mates, how to budget, and so on. The most important thing I learned though, was about my identity: the Adriana who wanted to be herself, yet who was stuck in the past.

It's not that normal not meeting your real parents, I mean you always have questions about yourself and society sometimes makes it harder. The sooner you don't care so much about what others think, things become much easier.

As you can see Australia means a lot to me ...

In my last months in Australia I traveled until I reached Tasmania. I went to some places by myself, and to others with friends. I went to Byron Bay with Bruna and Laura, my best friends! Bruna is Brazilian and now is heading to Barcelona and Laura is from Switzerland. We have the same views of life and happiness, and we were luckily in the right place to celebrate our friendship. We had our soundtracks (500 miles, Wonderwall, Red Wine) and we wrote a letter with our expectations for the next 5 years. We decided to open it together in a common place, we still don't know where, but it's getting closer. I already can say that things changed a lot from that time. **After Byron Bay we took different paths.**

I went to Melbourne and stayed with a few friends, more specifically with Andrew, a friend of my Aussie family. We developed feelings for each other and it was exactly at the end of my trip, so **I left Australia with a big question mark in my heart.**

I went back to my country in August 2003 and started my life again. It was a little hard and confusing. I was now back in my old environment with my family and best friends.

I love my country, but I have to point out that it is still far different from Australia in terms of quality of life and open-mindedness. As far as quality of life goes, we have a few people with lots of money, the biggest part of the population is really poor, and the middle-class working hard to have a comfortable life. Anyway politcs here is a big and shaming issue!

I feel half Brazilian, half Australian! I like soccer, so I like Australian Rules and surf. I still have to learn how to balance my body on a board. It's something (I don't know when!)I still will have to do. *Blue Crush* fitted in somewhere!

I went back to my work in the doctor's office and in the English school. I started to work like crazy; I was broke, I had to budget and make money again, even invest in my professional life again, looking for other opportunities and taking more courses.

I received three international visitors from my staying down under. Laura and Laila from Ticino, Switzerland, and Bianca from Sydney. It's awesome to go to the airport and pick up my friends. I love to plan activities, show my city, and hang out with my family.

Bianca's case was funny and atypical. I hadn't met her before she arrived. Andrew met her and gave her my email to be in touch with me and catch up in Brazil. We emailed each other for about one month and she came. She stayed with us three weeks and we became friends for life. I showed her our paradise, Ilhabela, and helped her to find a good place for surfing, the stunning Florianopolis!

My mum doesn't speak any English, and Bianca doesn't speak any Portuguese. At the end of the day when I arrived from work, they both could tell me stories about them. SO: If we want, we communicate even not knowing a language.

These experiences have been priceless. I feel great about exchanging cultures and meeting new people. I always try to see life from a different and spiritual way.

Last January, to my happiness and surprise, Andrew came to visit me in Brazil. It was amazing! We spent a very good time together. We went to Ilhabela, three hours North from São Paulo, and Arraial D'Ajuda in Bahia. We started a relationship and decided to stay together ... We chose Australia ... He left Brazil, it was very sad, but we knew that it was just the beginning. We sorted out all the visa stuff again which took about three months, it was hard to be on the other side of the world apart from "the" someone. **I left my job, family, and friends again, in the name of love this time.** It wasn't that easy but I had to give it a go for not regretting in the future, I had to have the answers for my inner question. It was very important to me!

Unfortunately things between us didn't work out, and it is still something difficult to talk about. I lived with him in Melbourne, visited Bob, Mary-Anne and Elle in Brisbane, and Bianca in Sydney, then decided to go back home. Even if things had worked out, I was supposed to go back to Brazil in September to be Lili's bridesmaid.

I never thought these things were going to happen in my life ... I can say I have stories to tell, and lessons learned to exchange in the future. For this, I told you I felt like writing a book, and that all I lived seemed like a movie.

We never know what can happen tomorrow.

Art is the best way to make yourself feel better. When I have a bad day nothing else is as good as sitting in my room with my sketchbook and some form of material.

Just like today, I was in the worst mood and was so sad (just the normal teenager stuff - why is she mad at me, why isn't he talking to me as much as he used to) but then I had art.

It's so easy to get caught up in conveying feelings through any media - today we were using clay. The other great thing is seeing a blob of clay turning into something beautiful, something YOU have created.

2/9/05

It's weird how things change. If anyone told me a month ago I'd be going out with Callum and I'd be happy all the time. I would have laughed it off.

But here I am... I guess it has to do with your attitude. If I said to myself "Mel if you try to be happy and smile all the time then you will be" it would have worked.

Instead I just felt a bit sorry for myself and dragged myself down. Now the only thing I have to achieve to be 100% happy is the good body image. For teenage girls this is most likely the hardest but I'll give it a good go.

This morning I went down to the beach for a walk ankle deep in the water.

I was so deep in my thoughts I didn't even realise how far I'd walked.

I wonder why people cant just be, just exist, they have to have a good car, send their kids to an expensive private school and other things like that.

The happiest people in the world are the people who do just purely exist, just live life and admire the beauty around them.

If only more people were like this then there would be no war, much less pollution and just a ~~much~~ more harmonious existance for everyone

144 7/9/05

Today I was talking to my friend and he was being really negative and complaining about everything.

A little bit is ok, sometimes you just need to get it out, but this was our whole conversation.

I felt like yelling at him because his negative attitude was catching.

I wish more people were positive because moods are infectious. When you're surrounded by positive, happy people then you are positive and happy.

It just seems so ~~easy and~~ simple, but sometimes the simplest things are the hardest to do.

136/12/05

Michelle Slaybaugh

August 5, 2003

This evening at the bus stop ...

She looked young, but I wasn't sure how young. She was wearing medical scrubs, and had a bubbly toddler by her side.

I asked her if she was a nurse or a dental assistant. She replied with, "Dental Assistant".

I believe she was a bit skeptical about me at first, but she eventually warmed up, as we both stood there on Crenshaw waiting for the 210.

She began to tell me about herself and her son. The child was very happy although I did notice he had a large bruise on his head. I asked her what had happened to him and the young mother explained how he was playing and had fallen into the toilet! We both laughed.

She then went on to express that working as a dental assistant was not what she really wanted to do. She was just doing

this job for money to support her family
and her dream. She started telling me that
what she really wanted was to become was a
forensic psychologist, to study murders and
serial killers. I was shocked! She then went
on to say it would take about 12 years in
school to get to the level she wanted to
reach.
I was blown away at this point.

Then she dropped the second bomb:
her baby's father was in prison.
For what, I did not ask.
I gave this girl much praise. I even told
her that she inspired me to work just a
little bit harder. Just because she had so
many strikes - and yet she will go down
swinging.

I was almost in tears just listening to her,
and I believe she was really touched by my
words to her.

Finally the 210 she was waiting for showed
up. She scooped up her little angel and they
were off. No names exchanged, only ages.

She was only seventeen years old, with
so much past and still so much future.

"Faerie" Sam Symonds

En el hotel Posada Jouel.

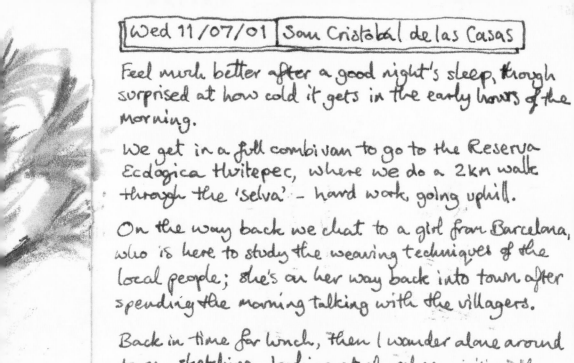

| Wed 11/07/01 | San Cristóbal de las Casas |

Feel much better after a good night's sleep, though surprised at how cold it gets in the early hours of the morning.

We get in a full combi van to go to the Reserva Ecológica Huitepec, where we do a 2km walk through the 'selva' – hard work, going uphill.

On the way back we chat to a girl from Barcelona, who is here to study the weaving techniques of the local people; she's on her way back into town after spending the morning talking with the villagers.

Back in time for lunch, then I wander alone around town, sketching, looking at churches, visiting the Museo de Arqueológica, Etnografía, Historia y Arte. Here I see pigskins that were used to transport the juice of the magey cactus to the place where it was fermented into mezcal. The museum building itself is based around a beautiful courtyard, and there are views out to the market, the ornate Templo de Santo Domingo, and the cloud-brushed mountains in the distance.

Have been thinking that I need to change my attitude a little – until now I've perhaps not fully thrown myself into the travelling experience, since I've been clinging a bit too much to attachments at home. From now on, I'll enjoy every moment as much as possible. And I'll just accept that I'll be eating Mexican food, and enjoy that too! Also, I'll feel I've achieved something worthwhile if I learn Spanish fairly well by November.

'Faerie' Sam Symonds

Just been reading Shane's book of
different accounts of Palenque and
hated the place when he came here
Wright, loved it in 1985. My opinic

The ruins are set in lush jungle; th
electric-sounding high-pitched buzz
means I can feel trickles of swea
I get through 1·5 litres of water in
Worn with time and footsteps, the
the temples looks almost as if it
out of the jungle. Now reclaim
we should imagine them as they
been in their day, painted bright

Of course the place is very tourist-o
romantic preconceptions of sitting al
cloaked ruin disperse with the mo
as the sun breaks through and hore
sightseers flock up the steps, and n
people lay out their pyrography-and
designs, and indian children try to
calendar symbols for 5 pesos each.

Back in Palenque town, there's not
apart from read/write, and wait
rain to clear away the humidity th
the inhabitants langorous, hangi
uninspired park. as if expecting
happen. This drawing is just my
splash of color in the park, as
English guys who evidently can't
night bus out of h

riting on Mexico. It gives two
ns; it seems Graham Green
; the other writer, Ronald
ewhere in between.

constant, almost
ts. The humidity
ing me, and
ning.
re of
own
grass,
have
arently.

now; any
a mist-
ist itself,
er
crafts-

e Mayan

to do
nevitable
es all
nd the
g to
n of a
some
t the

'Faerie' Sam Symonds

Plants on Contoy: the size of bushes depends on their situation; those on exposed ground grow low; those that are sheltered from the wind can gro higher. All of them help to hold the island togethe the dunes being the result of wind collecting sa against vegetation over thousands of years.

And something that holds me together is the wonderful fresh grilled fish lunch, with rice and guacamole. We watch the chefs cutting and cleaning the fish in the sea (the pelican has his beady eye on this too.)

We watch a they spread lash of salsa, tomato a onion slices, on the opened-out fish, and it between two grills to be barbecued. We chat a lovely Danish couple have been to Oaxaca a ...Cancun for meetings ... is a physicist She remarks o the 'empty comforts' Cancun - we agree that we have real comfort

154

Noticing dozens of little round shadows on the sand in the shallow sea, they turn out to be transparent jellyfish. They look like lace as they float, but take them out of the water and they become a lump of clear jelly in your hand, with spines running down them just discernable.

After lunch I have a few quiet minutes with the frigate birds, then a swim. A brief thunderstorm looks dramatic – grey sky over aqua-green sea.

Heading back in the boat, very slowly while passing alongside the island, so as not to disturb the cormorants on their rocky perch, we spot a school of little dolphins a few metres away, jumping in time with each other – not right out of the water though; just so we can see their dorsal fins breaking the surface.

155

Carly Anderson

1st November, 2004

Name: Carly Anderson
Age: 20 years old

I was happy, I was confident and I was doing what most people do at my age: going out and having fun! This all ended on November 1st – I went to bed only to have a phone call wake me up with the news that my big brother, **Luke, was dead.** As soon as I heard I questioned everything: how, when, where?! I wanted to call him, I then thought to myself, "No, this is all wrong". I'm going home to my family and sorting this out. **SHOCK …** I think it's labeled as.

GRIEF – MY NEW LIFE - Life after Luke   **22nd January, 2005**

Mum gave us each a diary to help express our sadness. I don't know why I was the last one to write in it. All the rest of the family did straight away. I couldn't for some reason, even though throughout my whole life I had been the one who had pen pals etc., when I was younger and kept a diary (which I destroyed for fear of having my lowest moments of growing up exposed).

I was the one who typed emails to you Luke. I was – and still am – so proud of "my big brother overseas" and I was always talking about you. I kept you up to date about everything that was going on with the family, with me ... (I'm so vain – actually everyone is they just don't know it!). So, why was I the last to write about my thoughts etc after you died? **I don't know . . . I guess I hurt so badly that I just couldn't write it down and I was still in shock.** For ages I wanted the people in the UK to call and say, "Sorry, wrong person" and then for you to call. **I guess it has been a slow process of acceptance.** Sorry for my lateness.

I promise you that we will try and carry on with our lives, but if we fall please don't blame yourself. It's just that everything we see reminds us of you in some way or another. Every breath we take is one that you haven't, and every day we live is another closer to you. After you died I wanted to die too! **I didn't believe that life would ever be a miracle or a blessing.** I believed it was a punishment of some kind that we were supposed to learn from but now I am starting to believe that we must go on and live for you as you were robbed of your life. **Since we still have ours we must live and take in the beauty** and try to ignore the ugly aspects of the world as I think you tried to.

DREAMS 22nd January, 2005

Luke, I have had so many dreams about you, it's just unbelievable. They seem so real at the time that sometimes my mind gets confused. Are you really dead? It sometimes gives me false hope, but at the same time I feel like I need to dream and contact you in my dreams just so I know you are there, so I can keep going. I've dreamed of a guy who looked like you and had the same body as you, who said, **"Look guys, Luke has sent me to tell you that he is fine and very happy.** He is at peace with himself and is watching over all of you, keeping you all safe". Then he walked away and I woke up. **I enjoy having you in my dreams** – it's the only way of contacting you. It comforts me when you give me a hug or just a smile so that **I know you're OK and I'm safe.**

I'm guessing that maybe you were answering my questions from last time I dreamed about you, when I asked if everything that we were doing, all the decisions we were making regarding your body and your belongings were right. So maybe you were trying to say, "Yes, it's all fine". It's as if you were saying, "It's OK to get my body cremated as it's not me anymore, it's just my shell – what I used

157

to be in. But my spirit has moved on like all spirits do, when they no longer have a physical body". **Am I right?**

9th February, 2005

Luke, It was our little brother's birthday today and we all went out to dinner and the only bad part about it was your absence. **I HATE that you're gone.** I must say life sucks. My family is all I've got besides friends and I love my family so much. It feels like whomever we love dies and for some reason, I don't feel safe any more. I hate living on my own. **I'm scared, upset, lonely and the only ambition I have is to find someone who loves me** and with whom I can have a family eventually. I want there to be a reason for me being here and I want someone to need me.

LESSONS LEARNED

24th May, 2005

Luke, I just want to say that a piece of my heart belongs to you. No one will ever take my big brother away. I just bought myself another inspirational book. After reading it I have found so much more hope and inspiration for what I call "My New Life". I have found that that I need to complete my journey and learn my lessons in this life. I really do believe that we are born again. **I feel that I have a lot to look forward to:** children, love, romance, family, friends, careers and opportunities. I have realized that I too will die one day and hopefully leave my mark on the world. I wish that all the members of my family could see that life isn't over just because one of us isn't here. **Luke, you will always be in our hearts** and there will always be sadness in our hearts, which will always belong to you. I will be twenty years old in a couple of weeks and that too contributes to **"My New Life". Good Luck to me ... and to my family who will soon be living by the sea.**

Where is my head at?! I don't know, living in the city on my own ... I can't get any work. I'm still struggling to come to terms with my older brother's death, and, sometimes I just find myself crying. **I don't know what to do!!!**

2nd August, 2005

I feel like I'm trying to get on with my life and try to preach it to others, but even though **I crave happiness,** I consistently feel as if I am consumed by sadness.

23rd August, 2005

Half of me loves life and wants to get on with it but the other half wants to stop the world from working and rewind to when everything was perfect and I had a complete family. **We were so healthy and happy.** I find myself thinking to myself, "You are twenty years old. **You can do it!** Complete your studies in business administration and at the end get a job for a year and then go on an overseas holiday with a friend or two. Then, fall in love and have a family".

How perfect and organized does that sound?! Of course I don't think everything will go exactly according to plan, as even though **I'm young all I want to do is settle down and have a family.** Even though I'm probably not ready in any way, shape, or form and in many ways my life is really just beginning. It's just that over the last three years **I have lost two grandfathers and a brother** and I sometimes think that I want to have more family members. I want more people to love and share life and laughter with! So I hope I succeed with my plans but in the meantime I need to get through my grief/growth etc., before making any huge life-changing decisions.

Carly Anderson

Hey Luke, You wouldn't believe it. I just got a job offer! It's just a Christmas casual job at a discount retail store but who cares?! I've been trying for a bloody year!
Anyway **I just wanted to say I'm having a good day.** I dreamed of you this morning just before I woke and although the dream was a bit weird, it was good to chat, even if it's not real. **I love seeing you and chatting with you in my dreams. So thank you for being there for me.** I'm going to go and listen to my fave album by Jack Johnson now! Love, Carls

30th August, 2005

I've been thinking today about how people act and treat other people. **No matter whether it is well-meaning advice and encouragement, no one has the right to tell someone else how they should react.** What my family and I have encountered in the last ten months is sympathy, care and advice. Advice – don't you love it?! Some people give you bad advice, some good, but what is most annoying is advice about which they have no direct experience to speak of. If they haven't had the experience, they don't know how we feel, how to cope, or what to expect so I wish that if they wanted to help they would just listen and offer comfort and happiness. Simple as that.

BOOKS

18th October, 2005

I just bought a book called 'Don't Kiss Them Goodbye' by Allison Dubois. So far I have read 8 pages and I have left two tear drops on the last two pages I read. What she writes about is so similar to how I feel. If I ever had a wish it would be for my big brother to be alive, happy and well and back with our family telling us all about his travels. **I want that so much, it hurts.**

Dear Luke, today is the anniversary of your death and **I can't believe a year has gone.** I'm still in shock and still not ready to let go. I may never be able to say good-bye forever but I just can't bear any more heartache so instead I tell myself how far I've come. I have still managed to live on and so have the family and I am so proud of all of us for doing that. I must say today was weird as our younger brother had to go to school for most of the day but returned home as soon as he could to be with us. So we just sat around in the afternoon for lunch etc. We had wine and cheeses and talked about you. **It was a beautiful sunny day, you would have loved it.** People dropped in to pay their respects and just to give the family support.

At night we had mum's homemade Indian curries that you loved and we toasted you with some expensive red wine, followed by some good white wine. You would have thought it was a good idea, I'm sure! Anyway we laughed, toasted, talked and cried today ... **all in memory of you!!**
I hope you enjoyed it with us in spirit.
Love, Carly

P.S. We also decided to sponsor a child overseas in your memory. He is a little seven-year-old Indian boy called Robin.

"If in the twilight of memory we should meet once more, we shall speak again together and you shall sing to me a deeper song. And if our hands should meet in another dream, we shall build another tower in the sky."
The Prophet, Khalil Gibran.

In loving memory of LUKE CHARLES ANDERSON, 1982-2004

CLASS PROGRAM

NAME **Brittany Ervin**   ADDRESS **Self Discovery Lane**

SCHOOL **Girlosophy**   CLASS **#1**

		PERIOD 1	PERIOD 2	PERIOD 3	PERIOD 4	PERIOD 5	PERIOD 6	PERIOD 7	PERIOD 8
TIME	from to...								
MONDAY	SUBJECT								
	ROOM								
	INSTRUCTOR								
TUESDAY	SUBJECT								
	ROOM								
	INSTRUCTOR								
WEDNESDAY	SUBJECT								
	ROOM								
	INSTRUCTOR								
THURSDAY	SUBJECT								
	ROOM								
	INSTRUCTOR								
FRIDAY	SUBJECT								
	ROOM								
	INSTRUCTOR								
SATURDAY	SUBJECT								
	ROOM								
	INSTRUCTOR								

fabulous!

poetic

iNDIVIDUALITY

NURTURING MIND, BODY & SPIRIT

inner girl
MY StOrY

Girlosophy 101.

Super

162

Sunday July 24th, 2005

**It's rough being me sometimes
&
I'm trying to get myself together**

Dear Diary,
It's really tough being me sometimes. I would never want to be anyone else because God made me this way and **I love myself, but it's just rough sometimes.**
I sit down and think a lot about different aspects of my life. Throughout school, I had friends and people who I got along with, but my main focus was my school work. I am 22 years old and I've never been kissed (even though I am in love now but we don't go together). **I've never had a big social life.** I have some best friends and good friends, but most of us are so different and we are all busy with our own agendas, so we don't get to hang out much.

Lately I have not talked to that many people because **I don't want to burden anyone** with my thoughts and feelings, so I just talk to God about it. That helps a great deal and so does **writing in my blogs and writing my poetry.** At my retail job, I only get 10-15 hours per week, so that got to me a little bit, but I manage.

I still stay with my mom and we had one of our talks and she said I am a smart person and she thought I would be doing more with myself by now. Most of my family really wants me to go back to university or to try community college. **I don't know how to handle work and going to school at the same time.** It's too much for me. I tried college right after I got out of high school for two-and-a-half years. I dropped out in early 2003 because the expenses were too much and I didn't want to take out a ton of loans. **I really want to go to broadcasting school** but it costs $13,000. If I could just go to school and not worry about expenses and not work, I would be able to focus. My mom wants me to

163

get myself together completely and move out. **I am going to try my hardest** to move.

- DIDN'T FINISH THIS ENTRY - sorry!

Journal Entry ...
Saturday, February 18, 2006

- What's up with me? I have to get it together -

Okay, **do I take my self too seriously?** Am I too bold for my own good? I had a crush on this guy named Brandon who helped me with getting my new phone. Well, I mustered up some courage and on Valentine's Day, I sent him a text message reply after he'd answered a question about my phone and told him that I had a crush on him. I didn't get a reply back, but (come to think about it) who would send a message back to someone they met a week or two prior saying that they had a crush on you? But then again, what is the harm in that? My cell phone bill was almost $100 and I was wondering why I was charged so much, so I gave Brandon a call and left a message about it. He didn't return my call about why I was charged the amount. So I called the store and they answered my question. I think I really slapped myself in the face with this one. He probably thinks I'm crazy. **I don't want to make assumptions,** but what else can you think about this situation? What can I say but that I put my own foot in my mouth.

To top it off, I haven't been working on my writing or my projects like I should. My spirits have been kind of low and my morale has been kind of down. I've even gotten a little depressed. I think a major part of it is because I don't go out too much and I really don't hang out with anyone. I am so sheltered. I'm only 22 and mostly everyone in my age range or people that I know that are a tad bit older than me have families to support, married, working all the time, going to school full time, or all of the above. Don't get me wrong, **I'm happy for everyone that is doing well and I pray for their continual blessings and happiness.** I just thought this was the age where you're supposed to socialize and have fun. I really haven't experienced any of that. I'm not talking about drama, but authentic fun. **I don't get to socialize much at all.** I have my family to talk to, but they have their own things to do and I realize that I'm grown and I need to do my own things. **God is the only source that holds me together when I'm down.** God is a blessing. Thank goodness God will never leave or forsake you.

Lately, all I really look forward to is going to church and my normal daily routine (work-home-naps). God is definitely trying to pick me back up, but I know I have to reach deep in myself and re-evaluate myself and step it up if I want things that I've started to work on to happen. **Sometimes I do wonder what it's like to have a boyfriend** because I've never had one, but I also know that boyfriends most of the time are not what they are cracked up to be and that is not where your happiness 100% lies.

Happiness is keeping all of your trust in God and being happy with yourself completely. I still don't feel completely comfortable at my new job. I do socialize with a couple of people on a regular basis and I am so thankful that the drama is limited, but a lot of times I feel just by myself there. I worked with very seasoned co-workers. Most of them have been in their field for a long time, so **I'm the youngest who works there.** It can be pretty rough when you don't work around anyone who is your age range and a bit intimidating. I do enjoy talking to some of them and I think that they are very knowledgeable. I think from time to time the boss has tried to see what buttons she can push with me because I'm the youngest perhaps. On another note, I do think that they've tried to make me feel welcomed.

Brittany Ervin

It's just me; I need to work on some things within myself to learn how to adapt better and to relax a bit more. To top that off, I made a huge mistake at work a couple of weeks ago. I erased all of these orders on the computer by accident. They asked all of us the next week who was responsible for it. I told them I did it, but that it was unintentional. I felt so horrible about it that I was really stressed that entire week and my whole body ached and I had headaches. **I've definitely learned my lesson** about that ordeal at work and also not to ever stress myself out like that ever again regardless of the circumstances. **I guess my new job is taking longer than I thought to get used to.**

Lastly, I went to browse around at my old job to see what I could find to buy and I talked to some of my old co-workers. One of my former co-workers that I confided in quite a bit when I worked there didn't speak to me when I said hi to her. She had to see me. I was standing practically next to her and she just kept walking. **That kind of sucked.** I don't want to make assumptions about it, but if she really was ignoring me I can only think of one reason why. I remember her saying at Christmas time a few years back that if I gave her a Christmas card to not give her a religious one because she hated religious ones. I sometimes send her religious emails and if she still feels that way that could be why she completely ignored me. **If that's the case, I think that it's crazy,** but like I said I don't know that for sure, but that could possibly be the reason.

So right now I'm having my emotional ups & downs, but I want to build my spirituality with God even more, so I can be even stronger.
I know this lady who is a fashion designer and she looks like she is about in her 40s and she doesn't have any kids, and no husband and she is totally rockin' it with her fashion business and happy.

166

I want to get to a point where my inner strength is at that level.
I am thankful for God and my family. That is a pheno-
menal blessing in itself which I'm very humbled about.
It's not always easy when something you do slaps you back
in the face or when you feel down. If you learn lessons
from certain things you do, that is what counts. But am
I wrong for telling Christian I love him? Am I wrong for
telling Brandon about having a crush on him? **Am I wrong
for taking that first step and standing up for my feelings?** I'm not
trying to take the matters into my own hands because it's
in God's hands. I just believe if you feel something for
someone, you better say it or you'll always wonder "if
I said this" & "if I said that". I think that after God
has led you to do your part, you should definitely leave
it with him and not try anything else and so I haven't.
I am going to pray to the Lord for me to get my spirits
back up, to stay content, to stay patient, and to get me
completely determined and motivated again with working
on my writing and my projects. **I know I can do it, but I have to
get more motivated and I will.**

AND THE WINNER IS...
Brittany!
dreams come true!

RESPECT
love GOD TRUST

Ashley Willcox

I awoke before the sun rose. It was a quiet still morning. Sarah and I sat by the fire as her boyfriend left for work.

"Let's go surfin this mornin!" she said excitedly.

I felt tired and ready to go home, "You know what, I think I'll leave now, cos if I surf I'll be even more tired and it's a pretty long drive..."

I left Sarah and her beautiful property, acres and acres of spotted gums and burrawang palms. It had been my heaven since I was a little girl and now all grown up I'd been so excited. It was the first time I'd ever been able to drive myself down to spend a week surfing and laughing with Sair.

As I drove along the highway I remember turning on the windscreen wipers as the rain gently sprinkled down. I wonder what I was thinking about as I came around the bend on the mad mile? Was it the boy who I'd befriended in the surf? Was it the freaky clairvoyant who had approached me when I had sat intrigued by the crystals in her hippy shop? Or was it my friends and family who I had so dearly missed? I'll never know...

My next memory is Mum sitting next to my hospital bed. It was quiet and dark but I didn't feel scared. I had on some brand new flannelette pyjamas and a little bear was sharing my bed. He had OUCH and a bandaid embroidered across his purple tummy. There were bandages across his head, arm and leg. Mum later told me I had named him Poo Leg because he had a little brown stain on that bandage. I have amnesia. At first I just thought it was because my body had decided to look after itself by blocking out something so traumatic. Though as I have learnt it's all a part of the brain injury I sustained at the moment of impact.

My car slid out on the wet road as it came around the bend. It twisted and flew up the other side of the highway. The four-wheel drive that was approaching from the opposite direction had no escape. It impacted my car on the passenger's side front tyre. The same tyre the clairvoyant had asked me to check the air pressure on. **"It means you have to focus on more earthly matters,"** she had said. I flipped the four-wheel drive onto its side and I must have head-butted my steering wheel. The whole engine was on the inside of my car. But somehow I escaped alive. As did the occupants of the other vehicle.

I have a tiny scar on my left knee. I was charged with negligent driving because it was my vehicle that had crossed the double lines. I have spoken to the policeman who came on the day. He was such a lovely man who was genuinely concerned about my wellbeing. "What happened?" he asked. "Do you remember being tired?" He explained that he had seen me on the day of the accident. I was so interested to know what had happened because the neurologists have told me my brain wasn't recording and **I'll never have the memory back.** "Well, you were mildly aggressive to the people who were trying to help you ... but don't worry we understood that it was a part of your head injury. As I always say, you can replace cars but you can't replace people."

I do have one memory though. Initially I thought it was a dream I had in hospital but that would have been impossible. The vision is just a glimpse of blurred color moving at an incredible speed and I can feel my heart beating at a million miles an hour.

In the last two days that I remember being in the hospital, I was transferred to another room with other patients. I remember making friends with them and there was certainly a lot of laughter except when I kept on repeating, **"I'm bored, I wanna go home!"** The lady in the bed next to me told me to shut up or she'd throw something at me because she was confined to her bed and was going to be there for a long time.

Not long after I'd left on that fated morning, Sarah said she had a horrible feeling about me. As she turned on the radio she listened to reports of a car accident at Mogo. She sprinted over to the big house so she could call her mum to say how worried she was. Annette had to pass by my accident on her way to work. She knew it resembled my car but didn't know my number plate so she pulled over and asked the policeman. I can't imagine how sick she must have felt when he told her it was a young girl. I was rushed to hospital and then I was airlifted to Canberra. By the time Sarah got to me I had been sedated and was all tied up in my bed ready to go into the helicopter.

I have come to value each day as a miracle. It is a blessing I am still here and I now say that I head-butted myself into happiness. While it has been a long recovery, I didn't feel I had any right to complain. I am walking and talking and had no broken bones. The only frustration has been my fatigue.

For the first six or so weeks I slept pretty much all day and all night. Mum said I couldn't handle anything but silence. Music, the television and people who spoke loud caused me to suffer. My friends and family were so supportive. **They treated me like an angel.** I especially have to be so thankful to my mum, Nola, who has been with me every step of the way. Our relationship has deepened so profoundly.

Mum always said that at the heart of every negative is so much positive. Even though you may not be able to see it at the time. Spending so many months alone during the day at home in bed, I have come to understand this. **It can be**

quite a confronting thing to have to sit with yourself. However, I now look at my accident as a really good thing and I can honestly say I'm glad it happened.

Finally I had been forced to stop, something I'd been wanting to do for so long but had never let myself. But in the process of not listening to my heart and having trust in the universe I was miserable. As a result of my accident I had to defer my studies at university and wasn't able to work for a few months.

I just thought it was God giving me a huge message: **that it's okay to slow down, and stop!** I'd been pushing myself to achieve for far too long, forgetting balance and to actually enjoy my life. There is so much beauty available in each day, but we can so easily forget this, especially if we're stressed and anxious. I feel like I've woken up to what Mum had always tried to get through to me, **"Thoughts are like clouds, they come and go. So hold onto the good ones."** It's a special way to look at hard times or any negative emotions. If you find yourself in a rut, it is so hopeful if you believe and accept that it will pass. As Marianne Williamson wrote, "It is not our darkness, but our light that frightens us most". It was the first time that I've been able to release some of my girlhood insecurities that had tormented me for years.

Each and every person has a special role to play. After focussing all my energies on my studies, I have learnt that others should come first. The accident has taught me how important people are. I have come to value my friends like never before and try to be there for them as much as I can. For we need to cherish all the beauty that we have. We are all in this together but sometimes we can get so caught up in our own lives that we can take for granted the importance of all those around us. **For we are all reflections of one another.** There were certainly days in the beginning when my body was releasing such a massive shock. I couldn't watch the news because the negativity would really disturb me. I remember that the London bombings had occurred on my second last night in hospital. Every TV channel was flooded with the pictures. I couldn't sleep that night.

Although it did take time, my memory and concentration has improved. I can even read books and most importantly, drive again. My results from the neuro-psychological test were extremely positive. The psychologist was thrilled when he gave them to me because he said that normally, it isn't such good news. While my capacity to retain information is still impaired I'm doing pretty well and I completely accept that my levels are below what they used to be. **I believe it all happened for a reason.** I just can't believe how patient Mum was. She said she applied her Buddhist practice when in the hospital I would ask, "What time's dinner ready?" "Six o'clock," she would respond. Then one minute later I'd ask the same thing.

I know I certainly drove some of my friends up the wall when I kept telling them the same stories over and over and over again. It was all fresh for me. Some felt it rude to tell me I'd already told them but I said just to let me know. So there were certainly a few humorous incidences.

My friends have told me that I said lots of fruity things from over the phone in hospital. One such comment was: **"I like love it in here! I'm getting heaps of attention!"** Sarah said when she came to visit me at the hospital in Canberra, she had walked out of my room to talk to the nurse about my condition. She returned to discover I had been through all her bags and was holding the newspaper she had brought for Mum and Dad. The picture on the cover was of my car and the four-wheel drive. "Sair who kicked my car?" she later told me I had asked her.

I believe a powerful force carried me through and helped me to finally see my own innate beauty. I had such strength and courage even when the neurologist had told me I couldn't have baths or go swimming for the first few months because there was a slight chance I could have a seizure. **I knew in my heart that everything was going to be all right.**

I feel so blessed and fortunate to be leading and enjoying such a life. **I want the strength to always listen to and follow my heart because that's where love and peace abides.** Instead of letting my mind or silly thoughts overpower me, this no longer needs to be.

I feel like everything I've ever prayed for or visualised has happened so I want to keep doing it, working to make the world such a bright place. Most importantly I have learnt that it's okay to be yourself. **Let life be a deep let go.** See God opening millions of flowers every day without forcing the buds. For dreams can come true, without that possibility nature wouldn't incite us to have them.

Blogging on

Weblogs or "blogs" are to the 21st century techno-chick what bling-bling is to J.Lo. They go hand-in-hand. **Stating who you are, what you think and what you're all about is the purpose of a blog.**

Some people use a blog to let their friends and family know what's been going on in their personal corner of the world (and, of course, whoever else wants to read it and make a comment!).

I know of one family, comprising of an impressive and extended number of half-brothers and sisters, step-mums, father and cousins, who all use a joint family blog to keep in touch with everyone regularly. Some live in the United States and the others live in Australia and New Zealand, so the isolation that distance can bring is obviously a great incentive to keep in touch, not to mention the avoidance of long-distance phone bills! Friends are invited to tune in as well to check out the latest news, escapades or musings and images which are posted by the tribe. It's truly a family affair!

It's an interesting thing that so many people want their life to be lived out loud and in the public arena. Perhaps it's a legacy of reality television. For older generations (parents, grannies, etc.) it's a completely new concept in so many ways. It would seem bizarre to them, to be so public about things that they would deem private matters!

In defense of blogging, provided it does not hurt or defame anyone (and, having said that, you should be very careful what you put on a blog if you mention other people or any subject that might be sensitive), it can be extremely positive.

Blogging opens up the personal to universal applications. Sharing is caring. When you go a-blogging you may find millions of like-minded souls out there on the web who really appreciate your sense and sensibility.

In my view, that can be a very good thing in many respects. It can be a way to include those who you care about in your world, even if you are far away you can let them in to a level of intimacy and knowledge that maybe will serve to enhance your relationships.

Writing on a blog how you feel – especially when it is to congratulate someone or applaud a milestone – can show them how proud you are of them (for them!). It shows that what they do matters.

For the purposes of writing, if you prefer to type than handwrite things, then a blog may be the best kind of journal or diary for you. You may find it easier to maintain a blog and therefore to write something regularly if you generally go online to check emails and traipse the Net etc.

girlo blogs on!

I created a blog while I was writing this book. In the interests of not boring girlo readers senseless, however, I have not printed it here. I called it "Girlo Blogs On".

Over the course of the months of writing, it actually became a really useful tool and something that I began to love to do. If I felt stuck at any point, I'd simply go and blog it out! It really got to that point a few times. Sometimes all I had to do was blog for a few lines about something unrelated to the book or manuscript and then it would trigger me into a new area and I was back to the book again before I even realized it.

Maybe it was relaxing for a short time, letting me off the performance hook: "It's just a blog, let it rip!" Or perhaps it was just enough of a distraction to let whatever needed to come out to be released.

I found it particularly useful whenever I felt that what I was writing was too contrived or tight. Sometimes I was simply trying too hard, with certain parts of the manuscript. That's a true confession!

Sometimes the blogs are about the scale of my project and my inability to "crack it", or they are about my frustration of not being able to have a normal social life for a long period. Sometimes they show me all the little habits I have which (rather creatively) allow me to not do my work.

I just had to keep reminding myself that you can't force creativity. Forcing it to reveal itself only makes things more entrenched. For me, on this particular journey, blogging became the Great Un-blocker.

But I offer the blogging technique to you not only as a means but as an end too. Blogging can potentially help you to find the voice that is yours, it can help you gain confidence.

If you don't like it, you can always use the delete button!

Creating a blog may be the catalyst to write about and deal with things you have long put off. It may even give you closure.

Places to go on the Net
to encourage, enthrall and enliven!

Welcome to the Blogosphere! There are many destinations in the world of blogging and, at last count, over 27 million blogs or online journals exist on the web. From the general (to get you started) to the special purpose (to inspire you). Here I've handpicked a few, for your viewing pleasure.

www.daneldon.org

The memorial website and contact point for the legions of friends, family and supporters of gifted photographer and artist, Dan Eldon. Eldon was the youngest Reuters photojournalist at 22 years of age. He was killed in Somalia while covering a story there. He was an avid journal-er and his 17 journals truly reveal this artist's life. Be humbled and uplifted.

www.salon.com/blogs

The blogging section on Salon comprises some of the most intelligent blogs around. They often have terrific links too. My favorite blogger? "Struggle in a Bungalow Kitchen" – insightful musings and lashings of quotes. It always leaves you wanting more.

www.blogspot.com

A good general blogging site that has a neat design for you to create your blog, and if you have a site there, you can require people to register before they post comments on it. Handy.

www.mythsdreamssymbols.com

I love this site. Apart from the Sanskrit chanting of monks and the cool flash of a Tibetan Prayer Wheel floating up through the homepage, this site has plenty to get you thinking about while you write in your dream journal. Mystical and practical.

www.thenakedsky.org

A travelblog that is designed to look like an in-flight magazine. Cool anecdotes and tall tales – these boys certainly get around. Take off!

www.notesfromtheroad.com

A travelblog to envy. This gorgeously stylish blog will delight and amaze both the experienced and armchair traveler alike. Erik Gauger travels light and far, posting articles that are whimsical and insightful as he goes. Sigh. The photos are also top drawer.

"I draw the maps with a Micron .005 pen, watercolours, pantone pens, acrylics and pastel chalk crayons on Bristol paper. I write my notes with a small moleskin journal, and I carry a small bag."
Erik Gauger, from Notes from the Road

www.baghdaddiaries.com

The stated purpose of this online collaborative journal is "to return the dialogue about the war in Iraq and The War on Terror to a public forum". This site aims to make the statistics of military personnel killed in Iraq personal, and each hard-bound diary represents a member of the military who has died in Iraq. View the journals and be moved.

"A Diary conveys a certain sense of intimacy where we can offer an honest introspective dialogue and confess our hopes and doubts. As each diary passes from person to person, perhaps we'll find out we have common hopes and doubts, regardless of where we stand."
The Baghdad Diaries Project,
1000 Journals, www.baghdaddiaries.com

www.rebeccablood.net

What's in Rebecca's pocket? The Blogging Queen trawls the Net for What You Need To Know and writes about it neatly. Enjoy pop culture meets Lit Girl. Even better she's written the definitive book on the subject: The Weblog Handbook: Practical Advice on Creating and Maintaining your Blog (Perseus Publishing/www.amazon.com). Now you have no excuse!

8. Last words & words to last

Freedom of expression (me on my soap box)

Many people say that the Pill and feminism in the early 1970s were the turning point of the 20th century. In the name of freedom, sisters began doing it for themselves and in many ways that change is still sending shockwaves around the globe. Like any revolution worth its underwire, there were some pretty extreme moments, but that is not to say it wasn't, at the heart of it all, correct in theory.

How do we know? We sit today in the 21st century and life as we know it bears little resemblance to the days of 40 years ago. The Baby Boomers may be older but so too is Generation X. Now Gen Y comes forth and the Internet is the new connection for us all. As females living in the West, we take for granted that we can be educated to the highest levels if we so desire, get a job and work for decades, marry – or not; have children – or not; clean the kitchen – or not; become an explorer, or whoever we decide we are destined to become.

The choices have been extensively widened concerning what we can now do with our lives. We do in fact have freedom of expression regarding our life choices – if we choose to believe it and act upon it.

So how then can we best express ourselves? Rebellion is overrated and anger only begets more of the same. Without having an answer that is not a cliche I would like to suggest this:

WE SHOULD EXPRESS
OUR SELVES CREATIVELY.

As women, we can and should express our Selves creatively. If our lives are the sum total of our choices – or as it is said, how you play the hand you are dealt – then we owe it to our Selves to use each day creatively to ensure we don't limit ourselves with our thinking or by not taking opportunities for growth as they are presented to us.

And that's why writing can be so incredibly powerful and helpful in making sense of our lives and propelling us forward. On the page you will look and sound exactly as you are. All your insecurities, negative or skewed thinking, all your hopes, dreams and desires will be there, but they are ready to be transformed into a better version of reality. They can be transformed from the page or screen into a better version of you in real life.

We choose and shape our reality – our life experience – through our thoughts, words and deeds. Which, let's face it, can seem as though it is smoke and mirrors, or Snakes and Ladders, much of the time! However, if we wish to learn from our lives, and particularly if we wish to progress, it will obviously be in our favor to examine what those thoughts, words and deeds are. What is our motivation? What is our intention? Do we want the best for others? Or do we want it mostly for ourselves? If we spend time considering these questions, our choices, the options and consequences, and examine them against our present position, we will surely reap a better experience in the future. **Writing can give such perspective. In an era of instant gratification, it is invaluable.**

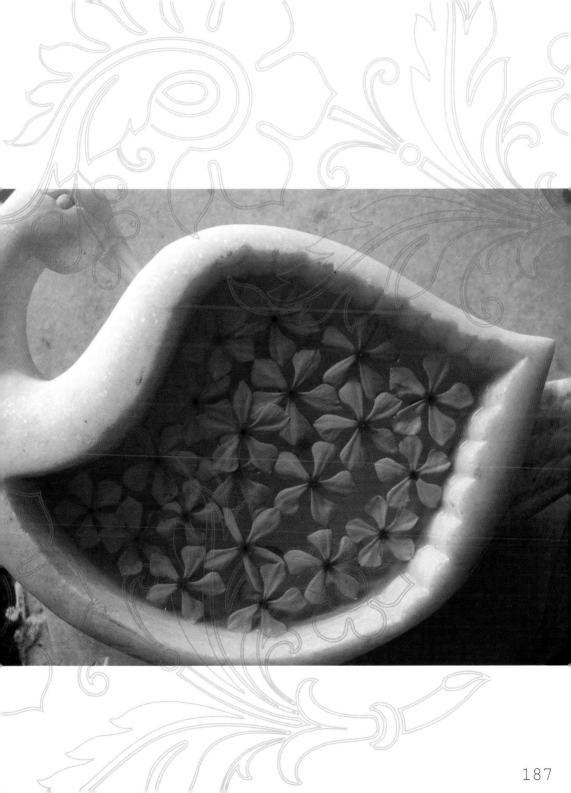

You can make a difference

(aka be the change you want to see in the world – Save the Whales, ... the Flowers, ... the Children, ... the Forests, ... the Dancing Bears of India, etc.)

All those musings, so little time! One of the ways not only to make your voice heard, but count, is to write to people, organizations and governments about the causes and issues you feel strongly about. Give a voice to those who may not have one.

If you want those in charge to know how we feel about the state of things (especially if we feel passionate about the cause) you need put pen to paper or keystroke to screen. You need to make it happen by telling someone how you feel. You need to back yourself.

Writing is ammunition. To be effective, it should be used carefully, targeting exactly who needs to hear what you have to say - politely. One of the reasons why the Save the Whales Campaign has been so successful in Australia is because schoolchildren have been writing letters to the prime minister's office for decades!

Things don't change if people don't make them change. As Ghandiji said, "Be the change you want to see in the world".

So don't whinge about things. Write about them.
To see change, you have to take the first step.

girlo Library

This is a very brief overview of some of the most helpful and/or enjoyable books I have read in the past few years. This is by no means a definitive list - some of the books are recent books I have finished and hence if they made an impression on me, they made this list at least! Others are classics - ones I travel with and keep on me always. A comprehensive list is included on Page 316 of **girlosophy** - *A Soul Survival Kit*.

For the Soul:
The Tibetan Book of Living and Dying
by Sogyal Rinpoche, (HarperCollins Publishers)
The Art of Happiness, A Handbook for Living,
by His Holiness, the Dalai Lama and Howard C. Cutler, M.D
(Hodder)

For the Mystery and the Beauty of Storytelling:
The Alchemist, by Paulo Coelho (HarperCollins Publishers)
Le Petit Prince (The Little Prince)
by Antoine de Saint Exupery (Harcourt Inc.)
The Essential Rumi, Translations by Coleman Barks
with John Moyne (Castle Books)

For Creativity:
The Artist's Way, A course in Discovering and Recovering your Creative Self by Julia Cameron (Pan MacMillan)
The Journey is the Destination, The Journals of Dan Eldon
by Dan Eldon/Kathy Eldon (Chronicle Books)
Griffin & Sabine, Vol 1-3 by Nick Bantock (Chronicle Books)

For the Feminist Within - Essays to Delight and Inspire:
Different For Girls, By Joan Smith (Random House)
No Logo, by Naomi Klein (HarperCollins Publishers)
I Dream of Madonna: women's dreams of the goddess of pop by Kay Turner (Collins Publishers)

The Hungry Spirit: Beyond Capitalism
A Quest For Purpose in the Modern World
by Charles Handy (Arrow Books)

190

girlo Gives

Girlosophy is a proud supporter of the Tibetan Friendship Group (TFG), a humanitarian organization assisting and rehabilitating Tibetan refugees in India. His Holiness, Dalai Lama, the Tibetan spiritual leader, is the patron of TFG. Please support this worthy cause. Help TFG restore and preserve the ancient and gentle culture of Tibet, and to support the Tibetan people.

Visit **www.tfg.org.au** to send a donation or to see how you can help.

 www.girlosophy.com